Trams on the Road

During the First World War women were extensively used to replace male crews who had
volunteered to serve in the armed services.
Dumbarton Burgh and County Tramways Company were forced to use women conductresses
and later they were tried as drivers albeit not with
very great success. Three of them are shown here
on car No. 19 during training in 1917. Uniforms
were not issued until three months after 'passing
out'.

D.D. Gladwin

Trams on the Road

B.T. Batsford Ltd, London

ISBN 0 7134 6125 X

Typeset by Servis Filmsetting Ltd
and printed in Great Britain by
The Bath Press
for the publishers
B.T. Batsford Ltd
4 Fitzhardinge Street
London W1H 0AH

Introduction

Many hours have been spent by experts trying to define exactly what constitutes a tramway. The actual names of the operating companies did nothing to clear the atmosphere, with the Burton & Ashby Light Railway being an inter-urban tramway, albeit one that like a demented shuttlecock drifted off into the fields from time to time, and the Glyn Valley Tramway a real narrow gauge railway. Great Grimsby Street Tramways never left the roads, but its neighbour, the Grimsby & Immingham Light Railway, has always been regarded as a tramway insofar as both ends of the line ran along the roadside. The Wolverton & Stony Stratford Railway was really a steam-hauled tramway throughout its life, whereas the electrified Camborne & Redruth Tramway spent its declining years as a freight only line, carrying copper ore rather than passengers.

So I have taken the logical approach that if it looked like a tramway, behaved like a tramway or even smelled like a tramway then it was a tramway. And the smell really was quite an important factor, for apart from the tang of static electricity, of leather, of warm metal and, towards the end, the bitter-sweet mustiness of decay, tramcars always had a warm reassuring sort of smell, quite unlike that of any other vehicle.

The box-like double-deck electric tramcar was almost unknown outside of the British Isles although where our influence was paramount, hardly surprisingly, we exported our own designs and so countries as diverse as South Africa and Egypt had vehicles that would bring a tear of homesickness to a soldier or sailor's eye. As far as Europeans are concerned, British trams have always been the odd ones as apart from a few Thomson-Houston operated concerns in the first decade of this century, the Continent historically always favoured 4-wheel, single-deck 20-seaters; unlike the UK where all passengers wanted a seat, continentals always left, and leave, a circulating space for standing passengers, a feature most obvious on modern articulated cars – those in Amsterdam seat 52 but carry 192.

But within the British Isles trams came in great variety and for the enthusiast in the 1930s, while it was a time of sadness as various of the smaller concerns closed down it was also a time of great excitement; almost all the larger municipalities announced their new-look models. Upholstered seating, high-speed motors and semi-streamlined bodywork all gave promise for the future.

The other side of the coin was observed by R.W. Kidner, the transport historian:

Many small systems were only provided with capital equipment once, when they opened, and when this wore out, they closed. One such was the Dartford Council's line in that part of Kent which borders on London – the Dartford Light Railways. Its route passed through the Rural District of Crayford, and at that time it was not possible to obtain a Tramway Order for a Rural District, hence a Light Railway Order was obtained instead. The system opened in 1905, but in 1917 all the cars were destroyed in a fire at the depot. This forced a marriage with the Bexley Council tramway, and their cars were used with some old L.C.C. [London County Council] ones purchased to make up. Things went smoothly under a Joint Council, and Dartford cars worked over the Bexley system to the L.C.C.T. [London County Council Tramways] at Plumstead; but by the Thirties the cars and track were in a terrible state. The cars moved slowly in a series of crabwise lurches, sometimes hitting a dropped joint and rocking for-and-aft as well. The motors groaned; the pointwork was worn and trams entered slowly and uncertainly. Some loops were well spaced, and the driver peered into a sort of bird's nesting box with a low-power electric bulb in it to see if a car going the other way had entered the section. All this was in marked contrast with the covered-top Leyland Titans of the Northfleet Tramways who had given up their trams and met with the Dartford relics at the lonely terminus at Horns Cross. In 1933 the LPTB made short work of the Bexley Dartford cars, and though given a short reprieve using borrowed stock, the line fell to the trolleybuses soon after. But the debt on the original capital was not paid off until 1947.

And we must remember, too, the good things about trams, their regularity, their imperturbability and their ubiquity. We must remember how cheerful they seemed on a winter's night with a promise of light and warmth. They appeared in Torquay, carrying great loads of holiday-makers, as much as they appeared nosing their way through the hotch-potch of industry, wasteland, fuming canals and busy railway lines that made up the Midlands 'Black Country' area. In Bristol Miss M. Welshman recalls how:

In 1910, to a child of eight living at Bedminster Down, a trip by tram was an excursion to paradise. Now in old age, I live again those magic moments on the swaying tram, clanking over its rail points – the driver bravely swinging his brass wheel and stamping importantly on his bell to warn of our triumphal progress. Sometimes, greatly daring, I would climb to the upper deck, fascinated to turn back and forth the wooden flaps incorporated in the seats for use in wet weather.

And the cars carried courting couples; couples so in love that the shape and design of their tram passed in a blur and only the patient voice of the fare collecting conductor intruded. The advantage of working for a Corporation Transport Department was never more obvious than on a wet Sunday when we could climb to the top of a Baby Grand on Liverpool's route 44 taking us away from the parental restrictions of Scotland Road to the solitude of Southdene. And how many lovers met on the Embankment in London and rode on an El?

Once on a Glasgow tram you could go 22 miles (35.4 km) from Milngavie to Renfrew Ferry for a few pence. Three-and-a-half hours of privacy. Or perhaps a day by Loch Lomond, which cost a Glaswegian one shilling and tuppence (6p) and most could afford that. Each tram-served town and city had a lovers' route and was none the worse for it. And then, too, the electric tramcar was basically a very safe machine. It is true they had accidents, sometimes even involving fatalities, they got involved in collisions, they got blown over, by the seaside they could even disappear under a flunder of salt water. While it is true that locally we had a girl with only one leg, known as 'Alice-who-went-under-a-tram', her accident had been a freak for somehow she slipped between the bogies whereas a Bristolian, J.E. Garrod, tells us that he, as a ten-year-old, wearing a cap against the bitter cold, was going shopping when

> A sudden squall blows off my cap, and the fear of damage to the cap by a tram rounding the corner, and the good hiding from my parent is the reason for a sudden leap into the road. I was carried along underneath the tram on a wire tray hastily dropped by a ginger-haired tram driver who was, to my astonishment, not angry with me. I was unhurt and carried on shopping, home then to breakfast and school.

Before memories fade let us admit there were dreadful trams, lurching and rattling along, sometimes with one end lower than the other so that you walked uphill and down dale as you collected fares, sometimes with flats on the wheels so bad they shook the frames with every revolution of the axles, then, too, the track would be so worn that bits of broken-off point blades lay in the sludge. It was not unknown for rails to twist in front of the disbelieving motorman and every so often a motor casing would judder over the granite setts and the lifeguard drop as some pin finally broke in half. Even out in the country there were problems:

> The cruisers and other ships on East Coast convoy protection duties often called in to Immingham and then libertymen for Grimsby embarked in a single-deck tram that ran at 20 minute intervals across open fenland. The trams maintained a service ferrying dockworkers and ships' crews and since the start of hostilities ran at night blacked out except for a single dim blue light in the interior; at speed the

trams had a devastating effect on returning libertymen filled with Grimsby ale. Interiors fusty dark and dank, suffocating with tobacco smoke, dipped and swayed, a ghastly motion often given an extra out of rhythm wrench by gales rampaging off the North Sea trying to throw the tram off its rails. Singing and roistering libertymen were silenced by the motion long before reaching the terminus at Immingham. Many a braggart shouting of his conquests among Grimsby women was turned into a helpless vomiting wretch.

That is one memory but there are others and R.C. Ludgate has described the most beautiful tram ever built:

> The Dublin Directors' tram was built by the Dublin United Tramways Company in June 1901 at a cost of £900 . . . But this was no ordinary tram for it was, perhaps, the most luxurious and elaborately decorated tram ever built for any tramway system in the British Isles. The interior of the lower saloon with its curtained windows as well as blinds had the twelve sepia coloured quarter-lights each depicting scenes of Dublin and was also fitted with comfortable armchairs. The top deck had 16 swivelling chairs and was enclosed by very elaborate and ornate wrought-iron work. Livery was blue and ivory with elaborate gold lining and the Dublin coat-of-arms on each side. No headlamps were fitted to the dashes at either end, nor was there a fleet number . . . a fixed destination display was fitted at either end of the top deck, bearing the word 'SPECIAL' – it is possible this was illuminated at night. When not engaged in carrying company directors on official duties or other notable dignataries it was occasionally fitted out as an illuminated [and] decorated

tram, touring the city system, in connection with very special events.

When you consider that an ordinary tramcar was finished in quartered oak, or sycamore, with embossed beading, with inevitably, plush velvet curtains and brightly polished brasswork, then what must this beauty have been like?

Even the most plebeian of trams was a thing of beauty and the motormen and motorwomen themselves were a distinctive breed for there was always some factor that made them quite different to the omnibus driver, a factor that spilled over into the trolleybus age but then disappeared. It has been said it was due to the harsh conditions and discipline of the great days of tramways, but how then was it so apparent in post-war drivers? Perhaps the answer is that a bus driver was just that, whereas a tram driver was at once an electrician, a mechanic and a fitter, had to know air and magnetic brakes, recognise greasy rails, dodgy points, often erratic power supplies and every day faced moithering passengers – in other words he had to be a versatile individual and accept responsibility. Perhaps this quasi-independence was above all why he or she was adaptable, patient, grateful to the management for any slight improvements – a canteen for example, or even when in the 1950s they gave us flushing toilets! – and always tried to be courteous and helpful to passengers. Truly it may be said the elimination of trams lost British streets more than iron rails. But tramway staff were not a dour breed for any driver or conductor of whichever sex, could always tell a fine tale. Old Jacko had been a Company Sergeant Major in World War I and used to tell us about his time in the trenches. One day the new God-fearing, teetotal, CO stopped the rum ration. The men who, after all, found facing death bad enough, objected violently to the loss of their one luxury, so Jacko went to see the CO. The CO asked, 'Tell me, Sergeant, what good does rum do?' and Jacko told how some weeks ago he had dropped a piece of rum-soaked bread on the dugout floor. A mouse ran out and ate the bread. It then hiccuped, balled its fists, looked Jacko in the eye and said, 'Right mate, where's that bloody cat?' They got their rum ration back.

There are still a handful of people who can remember the first trams to run in their town or city. There are also a good number who have melancholy memories of the last; this book is dedicated not only to them but indeed to anyone who feels some of the fascination of tramways. Inevitably the twin constraints of time and space mean a number of documentary leads could not be followed up and some photographs had to be omitted, always a regrettable state. It is almost invidious to name only some of the men and women who have helped in the compilation of both photographs and text for they embody a decade or more of research, one might almost include my driving instructor of many years ago – it's all his fault! However, I am indebted to William Kimber & Co. Ltd., for permission to reproduce the quotation on page 7 from *Jack's War* by G.C. Connell; R.W. Kidner, that doyen among transport historians, for patiently answering questions and supplying unorthodox illustrations; W.A. Camwell, Derek Coates, S.G. Jackman and Ned Williams who all assisted with specialized knowledge; Miss Lorna Smith of Torquay's Public Library who went to a great deal of trouble not only to supply illustration No. 53 but to sort out details of the original tram-shed; John C. Clayson of the Glasgow Museum of Transport who virtually supplied the caption to photograph No. 2 and Reg Ludgate who almost completely wrote the Belfast section for me. Photographic preparation was in the more than capable hands of a fellow author-cum-photographer, Kevin Lane.

I have pleasure in acknowledging the assistance of my wife not only in the preparation of the manuscript, but for permission to reproduce material from her unpublished thesis on the effects of tram transport on the lives of women.

Photographic Acknowledgements

Where possible, sources are gratefully acknowledged; many elderly illustrations bear no indication of their origin. B.T. Batsford 45, 99; K.A.F. Brewin 83; Birmingham Post & Mail 29, 122, 123; W.A. Camwell 23, 81; D.M. Coates 19, 20, 21, 108; M. Corcoran 68b, 68c; R. Crombleholme 94, 105; Croydon Central Library, Local History Collection 33; The late A.E. Dixon Collection 31; Dumbarton District Libraries, Frontispiece, 14, 101; J.H. Ellison 71; M. Fowler 47; Glasney Press, Falmouth 36, 42, 96; Irish Times, Dublin 3; S.G. Jackman 43, 60; Peter Johnson 30, 117, 125; A.F. Kersting 118; R.W. Kidner 25, 50, 57, 72, 76, 107; Kevin Lane 51b; Leicestershire Record Office 8, 55; London Transport 40, 74, 75, 86; L.R.T.A. 38; R.C. Ludgate 35, 61, 62, 63, 68, 69; Matlock Public Library 51; Motherwell Public Library, Hurst Nelson Collection 52, 73, 119; National Library of Ireland 12; Newcastle Chronicle & Journal Ltd. 46; The late R.B. Parr 78, 79, 92; H.B. Priestley 82, 88, 112, 114; Scarborough Public Library 22; George Shuttleworth 44, 91; Brian Standish 34; D. Tate 121; Torquay Public Library 53; Tower Hamlets Public Library 1; Peter Tuffrey 18, 37, 84, 93; J.S. Webb 13; Reece Winstone 32, 49, 97, 98; Woodspring Museum, Weston-super-Mare 95, 114; Woolwich Public Library 4. The balance are from the author's collection. If acknowledgements have inadvertently been omitted our apologies, upon advice this will be corrected in later editions.

Notes and anecdotes

Tramlines

Only four methods of traction achieved even remote popular acceptance within the tramroads of the United Kingdom. Each had its advantages and problems, the horse being prone to all the ailments of a living body, cable was extremely vulnerable as the slightest mishap spelled chaos, while steam, perhaps the method responding best to skill, suffered from the simple equation of weight to power. Because the track was light, the locomotive was necessarily light in weight and performed less well than it might. There were odd freaks like battery or petrol electric, compressed air, clockwork, and gas, but each of these required a technology far in advance of Victorian knowledge for the batteries bubbled and burst, the petrol engines stank and had a terrible thirst, compressed air almost succeeded but took too long to recharge and clockwork (which included a massive flywheel) took too much space as indeed did the motors and storage cylinders of gas trams.

The fourth method was electricity and this remains the transport power we must look forward to in the future for it was – and is – clean, efficient and reasonably economic.

Quadruped Power

Although appearing at first sight to meet the requirements of economic, smooth-riding people-movers, horse-trams were very far from an easy road to financial success. Pontypridd is a case in point. The population was about 32,000 and although the railways operated passenger trains, mineral traffic was so great that it took priority. The Pontypridd & Rhondda Valley Tramway Company received their Act in 1882 and eventually built just over three miles of tramway from Porth Square to Taff Street, Pontypridd. By 1887 the company, desperate to achieve some semblance of a service leased the works to a contractor, they retaining all fares (and logically supplying the conductors!) while the contractor supplied everything else, receiving $7\frac{1}{2}d$ (3.1p) per car-mile run. A year later maintenance was so bad that the company was fined £23 plus costs for dangerous trackwork. In 1890 it went bankrupt but having little choice the receiver retained the contractor, albeit at $8\frac{1}{2}d$ (3.5p) per mile. In 1891 the tramway was sold – to the contractor. The company had spent, in round figures, £20,000. The contractor paid around £3,000. The tramway still lost money but in 1898, British Electric Traction Company (B.E.T.) sensing a chance to add another tramway to their many paid £12,000 for the lot. They applied to electrify the line. Permission was refused and when in 1902, glanders (a contagious disease with swelling below the jaw and a mucous discharge from the nostrils) killed most of the horses, services ceased. A year later Rhondda and Pontypridd Councils, acting under provisos of the 1870 Tramways Act compulsorily purchased the whole system, B.E.T. asking £15,000 but accepting £11,000. Electrified, the tramway was still financially (although not in terms of passenger benefit) unsuccessful as although it closed finally in 1930, it was not until a decade later that the capital debt incurred in building the new works was finally paid off.

A rather tragic sidelight upon horse trams was made evident when in 1902 the Newport Council, who had recently taken over the operations from a contractor, declared that of 137 horses handed over, 21 had died and a further 21 had been sent to the kennels for dog food. On a rather more cheerful note they also announced that the sale of manure in 1903 fetched 8 shillings (40p).

Sometimes, whereas a horse tramway would slip in quietly, the very thought of mechanization in the form of electrification led to certain factions within towns or cities becoming positively apoplectic, as in the two University towns of Oxbridge where the battle between Town, who wanted more trade, and Gown, where the Dons wanted everything preserved in aspic, was won by Gown 2–0, with neither of the horse tramway networks being electrified but instead superceded by motor omnibuses in 1914.

It was legislation aimed at horse tramways that so bedevilled later engineers, for the original requirement that undertakings had to pave and repair the space between the tracks and 18 inches each side of them was due to the anticipated impact of the tram-horses' hooves.

The extent of horse tramways is often over-estimated but generally they were quite parochial affairs necessarily keeping to reasonably level routes; in 1876 there were 136 miles (219 km), a decade later 779 (1254 km), and even including steam-operated lines only 1040 (1674 km) miles existed in 1896. By 1914, 2530 miles (4072 km) of electric lines were in use plus no more than 100 miles (161 km) of horse tramway, the last London line closing a year later, it is said due

primarily to the seizure of its horses to serve in France.

Two examples of fairly typical horse tramways must serve for all. Paisley had a population in excess of 70,000 and for many years was well served by swift packet boats on the Glasgow, Paisley & Ardrossan canal who offered an hourly service to Port Eglinton. Steam coaches were operated in the mid-1830s but even the railway were unable to cope with the local traffic and a horse tramway was opened in stages until in 1889 the lines totalled 2 miles (3.22 km). In 1897 B.E.T. tried to purchase the system but fell foul of various vested interests. Despite an original capital of £20,000, accumulated debts totalled £10,000 and the Paisley Tramway Company were glad to sell up in 1902 for £15,000. The purchaser electrified the lines but sold out to Glasgow Corporation Tramways in 1923. In their 19 years of existence the horse tramway company paid total dividends of 89 per cent on their shares, averaging 4.7 per cent per annum, most profit coming in the years 1889–1891 and five years showing a deficit.

The Leamington & Warwick Tramway & Omnibus Company was, however, reasonably successful with their three-mile-long line, primarily as there was a positive traffic flow. Instead of trying to operate within a town, where other traffic impeded them and finding the paucity of passing loops made the journey little, if any, quicker than walking as at Paisley – 30 minutes for two miles (3.2 km) – this company ran what was really a mini inter-urban, taking 34 minutes for the 3 miles (4.8 km) between Leamington and Warwick. Life was relatively uneventful, dividends steadily increasing from an average 3 per cent (1885–1894) to a peak of 5 per cent (1896–1900) but in 1901 the company sold out their controlling interests to, inevitably, British Electric Traction, although remaining autonomous under their umbrella. Electrified in 1905, passengers carried jumped from 708,000 to 1,065,000, dividends then fluctuating between 1 per cent (1910) and 6 per cent (1920). The system closed in 1930.

Evaporated Water

Steam trams are, all too often, the forgotten story of tramways, possibly because their heyday was on services in the Midlands and the North of England. On a horse-drawn system in hilly country even a relatively mild gradient meant the addition of a trace or cock horse, who together with its attendant boy had not only to be provided but fed and watered, whereas the steamer required no such aid. The mechanical side of steam tramways has been covered elsewhere* but bearing in mind they were steam engines with all the coke fumes, oil and rusty water splashes and the other problems of this type of power there is no doubt whatsoever that hard work by the cleaners was required to keep them smart. Consider the fleet of the Bradford Tramway & Omnibus Company, 40 locomotives of three makes, 42 trailers with seating capacities varying between 38 and 67 to operate 17 route miles (27 km). And they were smart with the locomotives painted in maroon with white and gold lining and lettering. Window frames were cream, the wheel covers, or skirts, sienna (a sort of brownish yellow) with orange lining. Even the wheels which ploughed through all the horse muck and general filth of Victorian roads were painted in red oxide. The trailers were no less attractive with nut-brown rocker panels and stairs lined in gold and white. The roof was cream as were the

Steam on the Road, D.D. Gladwin, Batsford, 1988

window surrounds, vestibule front panels and the panels below the windows. Lining-out on the cream was carried out in vermillion. Trucks, sensibly, were black but dash and corner pillars alike were painted 'the deepest red from an artist's palate'. There can be no doubt that steam trams, however well painted, were noisy, as little or no springing could be provided; dirty inasmuch as coke fumes are always acrid and from time to time ash and soot would be drawn up the chimney, while escapes of steam frightened the wits out of the horses. Drivers too, had a sense of humour, the clang of the bell was normal but to wait until they were behind a little deaf old lady (who wrote and complained) and then to ring the 'Angelus' was not permitted! The Board of Trade had some doubts whether or not steam on the road was a good thing and normally only licensed its use for a period of seven years at a time and every engine used on the tramway was required to have a clearly painted number; a speedometer; 'a suitable fender to push aside obstructions . . . a special bell, whistle or other apparatus to be sounded as a warning when necessary and a seat for the driver of such engine so placed in front of such engine as to command the fullest possible view of the road before him.' Noise whether by blast or clatter was prohibited and 'the machinery shall be concealed from view at all points above four inches from the level of the rails, and all fire used on such engine shall be concealed from view.' In February 1881 a report appeared in the local press stating that the South Staffordshire tramways were to be operated by compressed air locomotives pointing out the quietness and freedom from smoke and sparks, compared with the steam engine, especially for the outside passengers. They never appeared but the steamers did instead! Moreover such was the demand for engines that in 1884 this company was still not operating a proper service, a council clerk stating 'There was difficulty in obtaining new ones [locomotives] the makers being overdone with orders, but the greatest possible pressure was being put upon them to meet the Company's requirements.' Perhaps this was why a report a few years later said 'they make a great noise and clatter, emit large quantities of smoke and steam. The engine drivers say that the engines are badly constructed and in bad repair and they cannot stop them emitting smoke for these reasons.' Whatever their disadvantages, though, in 1885 the South Staffs Company cars carried $3\frac{1}{2}$ million passengers so obviously they met a demand.

Acts of Parliament

Books have been written to describe the tortuous struggles between private company and corporation, between Urban Districts, or between rival promoters over exactly who was going to install what electric wiring and which tramlines were to go where. As a generalization, until the Tramways Act of 1870 a private Act of Parliament had to be obtained to permit building, and as neither Parliament nor the promoters had much to guide them, these Acts were modelled on those pertaining to mainline railways. In 1870 all this changed in so far as providing the would-be operator followed and fulfilled certain guidelines and accepted certain responsibilities then most difficulties were resolved. Most of the intricacies of the 1870 Act and succeeding Acts will be apparent from the photographic captions as they heavily influenced the very shape of the tramway on public highways.

The 'Mayor, Alderman and Burgesses of the Borough of Folkestone' were granted permission to build their own tramways including 'any offices sheds stables workshops stores waiting rooms or other buildings yards work and conveniences' and they were allowed to borrow money in order to do so. However, they had to maintain and keep in good condition 'so as not to be a danger or annoyance to the ordinary traffic' rails and roadway alike, being liable to a heavy fine for each day they were below standard. Their confirmation Act was dated 1901 and rather curiously for such a late date, regulations governing the use of steam locomotives were listed including a requirement that any engine arriving at a crossroads must stop in case horses were frightened. Fares too, were itemised (1d per mile for second class) and the promoters were disbarred from charging any higher rates on Sundays or public holidays.

Not unreasonably the proprietors of the Glossop Electric Tramway (the grandiloquently named Urban Electric Supply Company) were obliged to give notice prior to tearing up roads in order to lay the rails. In Worcester the proprietors were so long in finishing the works – one road being impassable for six months – that the site became known as 'the seige of Worcester', while the area adjacent to the Aquarium in Scarborough was unusable for so long that the tramway never achieved real popularity with the populace. London stood no such nonsense: 'The Company [London United Tramways] shall not . . . at any time break up any road or street . . . for more than half the width of the roadway.'

All enabling Acts stated the number of services to be run, usually every ten or fifteen minutes between termini, but rarely were they so strictly defined as for the Glossop Electric. They had to provide a service of cars 'for public traffic' from 5.45

a.m. to '11 o'clock of the evening', at half-hourly intervals. The penalty for not doing so was £5 per day, but some companies (the Glossop among them) in later years, as traffics fell, found it easier to pay this than waste electricity and pay wages. The Glossop system closed on Christmas Eve 1927. The United Kingdom Tramway Light Railway and Electrical Syndicate wanted to build a series of tramways in the West Riding but had to placate not only the county council, but the various local authorities who laid down their own quirky requirements. 'The Promoters shall [erect] an electric lamp of not less than 16 candlepower at each stopping point [and] shall within the parish of Glass Houghton use only hollow posts or pillars so that they can be used as sewer ventilators' were among others. Then too, the waterworks, an assortment of gas companies, the Lancashire, Yorkshire and North Eastern Railway companies (mostly rebuilding bridges at the tramways' expense) and various individuals joined in. However, the tramway could convey not only passengers but animals (horses were 1.6 p per mile), coal, coke, charcoal, cannel, etc., iron, sugar, cotton and, effectively, anything they wanted, rates for 200 or so items being regulated by their Act.

Not so in the then desirable watering hole of Weston-super-Mare. Their tramways were specifically disbarred from using 'carriages or trucks adapted for use upon railways' and the promoters (the Weston-super-Mare & District Electric Light Company) were not to run any vehicles other than passenger or passenger baggage cars on the lines. And so genteel was Weston-super-Mare that no trams were to run before 2 p.m. on Sundays. It was, however, even worse in Cambridge where an anomaly in their Act forbade any Sunday trams whatsoever.

Where there was opposition to the proposed tramway from influential people then the price of buying them off could change its whole course. It could even make the trams smell different in Coatbridge, for part of their enabling Act (so-called because it enabled the promoters to proceed) stated categorically that: 'The Promoters shall permit the local authority at all times between the hours of midnight and five in the morning to use the tramways for the conveyance of nightsoil and road materials in carriages moved by electrical power'. This was a rather extreme but logical price paid to placate certain councillors but undoubtedly reduced the rates compared with the multitude of horses and carts required elsewhere for this unsavoury purpose.

Three other factors contrived to negate the value of the 1870 Tramways Act. The first was the right given to Local Authorities to veto tramway construction along their streets, so even after the company had gone to the expense of obtaining surveys, their Act and the rest of it, some tinpot council could still say 'no'. Worse still, another provision gave the local authority the right to compulsorily purchase any routes that ran through their area 21 years after the company's Act and every seven years thereafter. Despite the provision for arbiters, the bitter truth is that a company after taking all the risks and building up traffics could be forced to take scrap iron prices for the rails and to sell the cars for whatever they'd fetch. The third unfair clause in the 1870 Act was that the tramway tracks were to be assessed at their full value for rating purposes. The situation changed for the better after the passing of the Light Railways Act in 1896. Intended to help improve traffic movement around the country by means of cheaply built railways, a number of tramway companies found they could adapt their plans to meet the Act's requirements. Advantages were many. The proprietors only paid rates of 25 per cent on their net annual value, could take five years in building the route (the 1870 Act allowed only two) and more importantly the old bugbear of road tramways, having to keep 9 ft 6 in (2.9 metres) away from the kerb (even if it meant they had to pay to have the road widened) generally ceased to be enforceable, for the Light Railway Act was envisaged as opening new lines through green fields rather than grey, sooty towns!

Power Supply

Often when a company was to operate tramways they included in their title the magical phrase '. . . & Electric Light and Power Company'. And electricity really was a somewhat magical beast because while the middle classes might know what electricity actually did, it was most unlikely that many knew how it was produced. The labouring classes, to whom a candle was an expensive luxury, found the earliest cars to be frightening, one poor soul even reporting to the police that he has been chased down the road by a flame-throwing monster. This was not surprising for relatively crude early overhead pick-ups often led to great showers of sparks and sheets of artificial lightning. This problem was never entirely eradicated and during both wars anti-flash plates were put over wiring junctions and runaround points to reduce the danger of keen-eyed Zeppelin and bomber pilots using these fireworks as a landmark.

Anyone who has had to put up with the dirt and smell of paraffin lighting will understand just how far the influential members of the town council would tolerate the trams,

even if they did not welcome them, in order to have an inexpensive (to the ratepayer) supply of electricity. Furthermore it was no great problem to insist on lights being fitted to each of the poles carrying the overhead wires, to give a rudimentary form of street lighting.

However, while town corporations generally avoided capital expenditure, it has been shown that company electricity could cost 40 per cent more per unit than when the corporation undertook the provision of power stations. Many, therefore, did so, including Swindon, home of the Great Western Railway, which after much procrastination finally got to work in 1900. A year before this the Swindon Corporation wondered whether to merely install electric light without tramways. The chief engineer of Portsmouth Corporation was asked his opinion.

> I would strongly urge on you the desirability of undertaking the combined scheme of light and traction. You would have the work done more cheaply than by doing the electric lighting first and the traction at a later date. Swindon is large enough for a system of tramways and if you do not undertake the traction for yourselves outsiders will step in and do it for you.

The power station was inevitably coal-fired and hence labour intensive, with normally one man handling the power output and a handful of stokers and cleaners keeping the boilers fed. The engineer (often, initially, covering the lighting as well as his tramway duties) was reasonably well paid, around 1900 about £300 per annum, where a tram driver received 6d (2.5p) per hour for a 65–70-hour week. (However, this latter was far better than the horse-tram driver of a decade before who had received £1 for a 100-hour week in Paisley.) Contemporaneous conductors received 40p a week and worked a 14-hour day, described by the Manager as 'the shortest in the Kingdom'. The Chief Clerk of a reasonably-sized town could expect £110–120 per annum; an Inspector, whose duties were very onerous and basically involved seeing that a fully crewed tramcar was at the right place at the right time come snow, sun or whatever, would take home £1.75 to £2.00 a week.

Obviously the amount of power generated varied according to the size of the town but until the coming of the National Grid and profligate wastage, town councils could take advantage of the simple equation that when tram services were busiest the lighting demand was least and vice versa. Typically, Swindon, population 38,000, with $3\frac{1}{2}$ miles (5.6 km) of tramway, initially expended £31,000 (compare with £300 salary of Chief Engineer) on a 600kw capacity installation; retail sales being at the rate of 5d (2p) per unit. By contrast the private Portsdown and Horndean Light Railway (a normal electric tramway) agreed to buy its power from Portsmouth Corporation at $2\frac{1}{4}d$ (0.9p) per unit in 1901.

Corporation versus Company

Swindon Tramways were opened on 22 September 1904, the Mayor stating that,

> Many towns of less size than Swindon have established tramways, and been able to make them more than self-supporting. The borrowing power granted by the Board of Trade for the construction of the tramways, which we are opening today, was £38,000 . . . this will be somewhat in the neighbourhood of the actual cost of the works . . . The interest and sinking

fund on this sum will amount to about £46 per week. The working expenses, wages etc. will come to about £60 per week, and the electricity used for driving the trams will cost about £30 per week, so that if the tramways are to be self-supporting they have to earn on the average about £136 per week . . . The tramways, of course, will be the best customer of the electricity undertaking.

As a generality the vast demand for electric tramcars in the period 1902–1905 sowed the seeds of disaster both for the operators and the car manufacturers. It was to both the credit and demerit of the latter that on the whole their workmanship was excellent. It was to their credit that the vehicles built when the tramway was first opened were the same ones, often substantially unchanged, that ran the last journeys 25, 30 or even 45 years later. It was to their demerit that such longevity destroyed any hope of development on a large scale.

Torquay bought their fleet (excluding secondhand purchases) in just three batches. Nos. 1 to 18 were Brush built four-wheelers which arrived in 1907; Nos. 19 to 33 came in 1910, almost exact facsimiles of the first series; and Nos. 37 to 42 were also Brush built, but bogie vehicles, in 1923–5. The line closed in 1934 still using all their cars. Six of the first batch were sold to Plymouth Corporation and renumbered 16–21 but, although not life-expired, were withdrawn in 1939 following the closure of many routes in the town. Interestingly the cars of the second batch (19 to 33) although only built three years later than the first were said to have been 'of poorer quality in both workmanship and materials'.

In some senses, what the engineer ordered and what he got was a matter of 'pot luck'.

G.F. Milnes were greatly respected as producers of horse-buses and steam trailers. Initially, they built on the success of their earlier workmanship but after opening a new works at Hadley near what is now Telford, used up their stocks of seasoned timber and ended with wooden bodies so fresh and green that Liverpool Corporation Tramways wouldn't have needed to paint them! One contemporary writer went so far as to declare that the sap was still bleeding through cut timber as it was painted. They cannot, however, have all been that bad for Blackburn Hadley-built cars of 1900 were still running when the system closed.

Most early electrical equipment was American. Dick Kerr (later known as English Electric, British Electric and United Electric) imported Brill trucks, Walker 33s motors (DK 25 type A) and Walker SI controllers (DB1 form A). Brush (lately Falcon) used US-built Peckham or Lord Baltimore trucks with Westinghouse motors and controllers. B.T.H. was the British offshoot of the US-owned Thomson Houston Corporation and G.E.C. started life as part of the General Electric Corporation of the USA. One difficulty throughout the life of tramways was that there were really very few tram-car builders, certainly when compared with bus-chassis and body suppliers, and those that did exist were either small or, while prepared to do the work, often too inexperienced.

In 1912 Mr Alfred Baker, General Manager of the Birmingham Corporation Tramways received just three tenders for the supply of the 50 complete tramcars of class 401, that from Brush was passed over due to Mr Baker believing that their electrical equipment was inferior in both design and workmanship. That of the British arm of Siemens was discounted as their work was felt not to be sufficiently proven, having only provided 100 or so sets of electrical fittings. Dick Kerr of Preston gave the highest tender but it was acceptable as Mr Baker, rightly, considered that reductions in maintenance 'down-time' (the time cars were unavailable for revenue duties) and spares would more than equal the extra few pounds. Even though Dick Kerr quoted for the whole works it is interesting to note that the bodies were built by the United Electric Car Company, trucks by Mountain & Gibson, motors (40 hp), controllers and circuit breakers by Dick Kerr, rheostats by E.M.B. and the very modern air and oil power-brakes were built by Cole & Partners to the design of C.J. Spenser & J.W. Dawson, themselves the General Manager and Engineer respectively of Bradford Corporation Tramways. Weighing 13 tons (13,240 kg) these cars, bearing in mind their narrow gauge bodies, seated the quite respectable totals of 24 downstairs and 30 in the upper saloon. Ordered in January 1912, they were delivered between August 1912 and March 1913, updated throughout their lives, but so good was Mr Baker's judgement on quality that they were not scrapped until late 1949 and then only because their depot and associated lines were closed. In their lifetime, 37 years, each vehicle ran over 850,000 miles (1.4m km). Where stability was possible within a tramway system and where the 'owners' (corporation or company) were reasonably enlightened a rolling programme of improvement to their tramcars was possible. Birmingham tramways were run thus. The whole concern was solid, with the family influence running right through it from the General Manager (father and son, 1903–1950) to the craftsmen in the workshops where three generations could work shoulder to shoulder. Always there was the emphasis on careful experiment, solid workmanship and durability of materials. Some improvements were obvious to the public, upholstered transverse 2 plus 1 seating instead of wooden longitudinal benches, modernized light fittings and air bells. Others, relating to comfort or safety, were invisible.

When open-topped tramcars were commonplace, top covers were tried in 1905. In 1909, after some difficulty with magnetic brakes, very efficient Maley track brakes were fitted where relevant. The same year a truck with two sets of springs ('empty' and 'laden') was assayed to improve ride comfort, as were later (1912) 'Parabo' patented springs. In 1924 no less than six variations on bow collectors were experimented with before getting the right one. As early as 1927 spray painting was given a test, but failed. From 1929 onwards, chromium-plated fittings in lieu of brass appeared, used ticket boxes were fitted on both decks and stainless-steel handrail sleeves were tried. In 1930 a precursor of the disc brake appeared and was experimented with, as were windscreen wipers. During this period vain, but interesting, attempts were made to deaden the resonance caused by the trolley pole and its' base vibrating on the roof; mainly by rubber- or oil-impregnated felt inserts. In 1948 'sandwich' springs of rubber and wood in lieu of coil springs were experimented with. Using helical, rather than straight-cut gears, reduced noise to a very noticeable extent, these being first tried in 1920. During the First World War a long trial was undertaken using single-deck cars towing a trailer. However, it was found in Birmingham that these units were slower, used more power and occupied more road space than the conventional double-deckers.

Fog lamps seemingly worked in London, so the Manager authorised the fitting of a sample in 1931. Although retained until 1935 no more were ordered.

And so the trials continued. In some ways the culmination could be said to be two lightweight vehicles which at the time, 1929, were unbelievably modern. That built by Short Brothers using alloys, where possible, and a light-steel bogie carried 63 passengers, was of excellent quality and saved 3 tons 3 cwt (3200 kg) in comparison with a standard car. The Brush-built car (843) on the other hand only held 60 passengers and suffered, as built, from severe flexing of both floors, probably as a result of excessive weight saving, some 4 tons 9 cwt (4500 kg).

Pontypridd, although sadly limited by available funds, tried to update their machines at least to the extent of fitting patent sandboxes (1905), fire extinguishers (1908), economizer power meters (1910) showing the amount of electricity consumed by each car and driver (the lightest-handed over a months' running receiving some gratuity); and rear view mirrors (1922). The value of top covers was always appreciated but so penurious was the concern (mainly due to the depression) that it took over six years to fit 14. But then the few staff had to contend with annual floods, subsidence and poorly laid original trackwork which left little enough time for improvement.

The Staff

In some of the photographs the uniforms of the men (and later women) are visible. Tramcar crews have always been abominably poorly paid considering the responsibility they carried – in effect they were regarded as an extension to railway staff – and like them as long as the uniform was respected then this to some degree compensated for poor pay and conditions.

The common definition of a driver was 'any officer or servant of the Tramways [Committee/Company] driving or helping to drive a car'. No demarkation here! A driver working for a big Corporation was probably just that, operating out of the garage with seniority a matter of great importance, a fairly rigid roster but a week of fixed hours. A smaller concern could not afford this, particularly where traffic was seasonal, three or four months having to pay for twelve. Weston-super-Mare, for example, had just five full-time drivers in January 1902 but supplemented these in summer (when a dozen cars might be in use) with permanent way-men, Inspectors and even storemen who had licences. Similarly, Rochdale used licenced clerks to work 'extra' during Wakes weeks and other holidays; the regular staff happily bequeathing them the non-vestibuled rattlers that normally lurked in the back of the shed! It is salutory to consider that Bristol drivers as late as 1941 still stood totally exposed to all weathers without even a roof. Open-fronted cars were, of course, commonplace elsewhere and indeed often when these were vestibuled there were bitter complaints of draughts and men going sick from neuralgic aches and pains. And draughty wasn't the word for it as the last trams went in the 1950s. There was little pleasure in standing with snow flurries building up by one's feet, sleet and slush from passing vehicles congealing on an already soaking greatcoat and frost in the beard. Windscreen wipers almost certainly didn't work well if at all, brakes were erratic due to worn linkages and to notch up sweetly was almost an impossibility. Issue clothing changed little in quantity over the years: cap, serge tunic and two pairs trousers, 'Melton' greatcoat, tie and, latterly, cotton summer jackets. Some delicate drivers wore shoes,

others serviceable boots, generally black although some concerns did not specify any colour. Mittens or gauntlets were vital. To see a man on a 1947 winter's morning take off his heavy motorcycle gauntlets, shake the blood from his finger tips, put them on again and resume duty was an indication of just how cold it was. Newspapers (or better, brown paper) under the uniform was usual. Pay? 1*s* 0½*d* (5p) per hour when the Manager got £1,000 p.a., plus expenses.

At the same time a conductor got 9*d* (7.5p) per hour. His job description on, typically, Bury Corporation Tramways included 'any officer or servant of the Tramways Committee having the charge of or helping in the charge of a car'. Known elsewhere as the Guard, a direct comparison existed with the railway Guard who, as late as October 1988, was still the person in charge. The job was no sinecure but was worthwhile enough that until the 1920s in many cases a newcomer would work without pay during the month or so he was training, while in the mid-1920s 10,000 names were on Liverpool's waiting list for jobs.

The Passengers

Generally speaking being a conductor was pleasant but hard work, although some workings were nightmares. Bury had a special tram prior to 1914 which carried the mill girls' babies to a town-centre nursery before 6 a.m.; drunks in Sunderland one day in 1930 pulled down the trolley pole – having climbed on the roof to do so – while in London in 1940 a conductress had her Bell Punch ticket rack kicked out of her hands and was (financially) liable for the loss. Football Specials were all foul. And it did not matter much where you worked, Portsmouth to Glasgow, Carlisle to Swansea, one byelaw was impossible to uphold: 'Any person who is in a state of intoxication . . . shall not be allowed to enter or mount upon the car', and if they did the conductor had to evict them. Try that at the Elephant & Castle, London; Scotland Road, Liverpool; the St. Paul's district of Bristol or Dale End, Birmingham, on a Saturday night!

In early days longitudinal wooden seats were normal in the saloon but some tramways tried putting carpeting on them to make them less inhospitable. Those in Birmingham lasted about a year. 'Any person who is affected with any dangerous, contagious or infectious disorder shall not be allowed to travel on or in the car,' said the Byelaws. The working classes, whose transport the tram basically was, suffered from diptheria, from jaundice, from tuberculosis, fleas, lice and other 'disorders' and they travelled on the trams. Varnished wood, at least, was hygienic. In Bury, again, Byelaw 9 stated: 'A person whose dress or clothing might, in the opinion of a conductor of a car, soil or injure the seats, linings, or cushions of the car, or the dress or clothing of any passenger or a person who . . . might for any other reason be offensive to passengers shall not be entitled to enter or remain in or upon any car.' Sand, seashells and seaweed were the problems inherent in coastal tramway operations whether at Torquay or Hastings. Coal dust was the South Wales problem and complaints were so many when the cars first ran in Pontypridd that within a few weeks it became the universal practice to run cars out specially for the workmen's services, only allowing 'dirty persons' on the upper deck, and having cleaners at the termini to sweep out any signs of their presence prior to picking up white-collar workers. As traffic fell, mainly as a result of the coal strikes of 1921 and 1926, the cleaners were dispensed

with, the conductors breakfast time being lost as he took brush and pan around his car.

Impact of War

The biggest 'if' in British tramway history is that if the First World War had not broken out would tramways have thrived, or at least lasted longer? Undoubtedly some would and some (badly planned, badly executed) would not, for the war affected trams just at the time when they were becoming more reliable, more comfortable and when all the defects of track, car construction and overhead maintenance were known and could be cured. Then, too, many 'company' tramways were approaching the 21-year clause in their leases. Some would have been renegotiated to give the operating companies some security or, if purchased by a council or corporation, would have been modernized, for in the circumstances existing prior to 1914 there was both security and a future for such activities.

West Riding Tramways were not one of the more successful concerns and in 1919 their General Manager said,

> In the past company tramways have been constructed and services run in districts that were really not ripe for development at the time the tramways were laid, but, in the hope and expectation of future profits, services in excess of public requirements have been run to induce traffic, and now when the period of patient waiting is beginning to be rewarded, companies are faced with excessive charges in all directions and their meagre profits seem likely to disappear entirely.

In 1914 drivers and conductors were the first to volunteer for the army and the first to die for many were Territorials. Typically,

500 Glasgow drivers and conductors were killed on First World War battlefields. They served in the 15th Battalion, Highland Light Infantry, of whom nearly 4,000 were tramway crew, a quarter of them joining up within 24 hours of their Manager (James Dalrymple) appealing for volunteers to form a tramway battalion. The platelayers, paviors and pointsmen who maintained the track followed them, some ending up working on the ammunition railways that operated behind the lines, while the overhead wiremen made excellent telegraphists. Men who knew the foibles of what were often quite elderly cars and kept them spick and span, the office clerks and the power station stokers alike, even when they were unable to join the armed services all too often went to work at the armaments factories which sprouted all over the countryside. Tramways may, as a generality, have offered security but the wages were so low that their moving was understandable.

Some tramway systems found their services grossly overloaded by movements of servicemen and with (horse-drawn) waggons carrying war material clogging the streets. Zeppelin raids were another problem for a few companies, while Scarborough Tramways had the ignominy of being shelled by German cruisers. Other tramways, particularly those at the seaside, saw their profits disappear like snow in summer. The lack of skilled men and of materials meant the cars, now virtually without maintenance, were wracked almost beyond repair. Non-standard rails became impossible to get and towns who had opted for the relatively unusual centre groove found it necessary to lift track from one line to repair another, while other concerns had to use their stock of rail to patch rather than re-lay a route. Little could be done to ameliorate the condi-

tion of cars, overhead cabling and trackwork, and many towns overcame their staffing problems by taking on lady conductors, but fortunes varied, Doncaster took on four in July 1915 and by April all were passed out as either 'motoress', 'motorwoman' or plain 'driver' according to which document you read!

But those men who stayed at home could be very anti- where women were concerned despite the fact that in, for example, Nottingham, preference was given to the wives of fighting men. Some tramway men went on strike over the employment of women and when the men in the trenches heard of this they said, 'Send them [the strikers] to the front!' One Lancashire driver applied his brakes hard whenever a woman Inspector boarded his car, sending her flying to the front end and conductors refused to hand her their waybills to check. In 1915, the tramway union in Bradford told the management that they objected to women being employed 'until it was absolutely necessary', but other places had difficulty in recruiting women. Chatham could not get them (and two local curates were taken on as part-time drivers), neither could Wemyss in Fife, where miners drove trams on a part-time basis after they had finished their night shift in the pit while Dundee, womanless, employed partially-disabled soldiers as conductors.

Women on Trams

One of the often overlooked social effects of the tramcar was an enforced change in, or at least modification to, women's clothing. In 1895 dresses fitted tightly over the hips and 'hip-subduing' corsets made natural walking difficult – women generally appeared to glide. Skirts were long besides being tight so that to ascend to the upper deck of a horse tram via the narrow winding staircase was difficult and impossible not to show a glimpse of black silk hose. A few years later the boring, unsightly underclothing of Victorian days had been replaced by a mass of frilly Japanese-silk petticoats trimmed with lace, designed to be seen as a lady in a billowing skirt (but still 38 to 42 inches (97–107 cm) long) boarded or alighted. Skirts, made of diaphanous muslin, cotton or linen in summer, serge, drill, velvet or tweed in winter, still swept the floor in 1900 but as a result of trams, and other forms of travel, became considerably shorter by 1914.

Equality was not thought of prior to the First World War and some managements having accepted the principle of women conductors and drivers tried to make their life easier. Women staff of the Croydon Corporation Tramways were provided with wooden stools on the platforms and canvas screens were fixed against the stairs to keep out draughts. Newport first appointed conductresses in July 1916 but they were used only on the Stow Hill route where the Cemeteries Committee provided lavatory accommodation at St Woolos burial ground, other routes having no female conveniences. In October of that year the General Manager reported that although he had failed to obtain any lavatory accommodation for the women at the end of the Caerleon Road route they would be able to utilise the premises of Mr Dawkins at Pill for which the company would pay two shillings per week – the sum of £13 had been allocated for alterations and fittings. By the end of 1917 there were lavatories available for tramway women at Pill, Malpas Road and the Market. Cambourne & Redruth first took on lady 'inspectors' in March of 1917, presumably on fare evasion duties, not

employing conductresses until May of that year.

Fears that women might be unequal to the job were, with a few exceptions, groundless. Ignoring bad language and unchivalrous conduct alike, they proved to the rough, male, passengers of Sheffield, Glasgow and other industrial towns that they were more than equal to the job. Indeed, in Rothesay in 1915, six female car conductors took the place of eight men who had enlisted and, in time, 71 per cent of drivers were female. Glasgow conductresses must have looked very smart in their Black Watch tartan, ankle-length skirts and navy service-type jackets. Such an outfit was considered to be a model uniform and worn with neat peaked-cap or hat, money bag and punch, was the basis for the uniform worn by women employed on the buses until quite recently.

In 1915 Mrs G. Duncan became London's first woman tram conductor and from a description of her we may be sure that she invoked the 'no swearing, obscene or offensive language; no spitting or any nuisance' rule which was common to almost all tramways. Housemaids, mill girls and waitresses followed Mrs Duncan's lead and by June 1916 the Paisley Tramway Company employed no less than 72 women. Their first lady driver, Miss O'Neil, did not last long as she 'could not stand the cold', but by September 1916 they had several other lady drivers, a lady Inspector and a number of girls on permanent way repairs. In 1917 both Paisley and Lanarkshire tramways sought to fill further vacancies but local lasses were in demand for war work so 30 young Aberdeen girls were imported. These girls, many being ex-parlour-maids or nannies, did not have the grit of the Sheffield and Glasgow women and only a few of them lasted more than six months as conductresses. A total of 376 female platform staff were employed at one time or another by Paisley reflecting the rule that no married women should be employed and the fact that the average age of female employees was 23!

In November 1915 the manager of Pontypridd tramways was authorised to employ women conductors at $4\frac{1}{2}d$ (6.7p) per hour; this was less than the men earned, equal pay being an almost unheard of concept in that era. Unsocial hours caused many to leave – in the six months ending September 1917 25 women handed in their notice.

On 24 February 1916 Weston-super-Mare tramways approved a proposal to engage women tram drivers – the first women drivers in the West of England – and although they worked until the end of war they were denied the five shilling (25p) war bonus granted to male employees. A three-day strike caused a re-think and an award of two shillings (10p) a week bonus for women was granted from 1 January 1918 as a compromise.

Dumbarton tramways employed conductresses from early 1915 but preferred to re-employ retired men rather than take a chance on women drivers. Eventually when lady drivers were employed, some refused to drive at night and others were unable to maintain scheduled times; one left her tram unattended and unfortunately for her someone undid the handbrake and the car, full of passengers, ran off on its own; another crashed her car into a motor-car, so, again, the company turned to men – discharged soldiers, some of them foreign, but all able to work long hours, anything between 60 and 80 hours a week being considered normal.

Although, generally, northern women were tougher, they too could behave in a 'ladylike' way. The General Manager, Mr Archibald Robertson, of the Rothesay, Greenock and Port Glasgow and the Airdrie and Coatbridge Tramways, was strong in his support of female staff. He claimed that Greenock Tramways were the first to employ female drivers and conductors and that the experiment had been an immediate success, the women having both the skill and nerve to drive a 12-ton (12,220 kg) tram successfully. However, he did not feel, in cases of sudden emergency, that women were as satisfactory as men would be and he cited a case where to avoid an accident they had acted in every way correctly and stopped the car, but afterwards (ladylike) fainted away! In 1917 James Dalrymple said that they were 'rapidly coming to the point where a majority of the tramway staff at Glasgow would be of the gentler sex' and that he would not hesitate to have the whole service run by women. He paid his women drivers 29 shillings (£1.4) per week – the same as men. However, tramway staff were generally accountable for any counterfeit coinage. In Newport in March 1917 a conductress had a bad two-shilling piece passed to her and when attempting to pass it back in change to another passenger she was reported and given three days' suspension, losing both the florin and three days' pay; another conductress accepted so much bad coinage that she received only $3s.6d$ (17.5p) at the end of her 60 hour week! In Manchester a passenger offered a conductress a matchbox for his fare and he, most assuredly, received in exchange the sharpness of her tongue.

In Portsmouth, although some conductresses had been taken on, by September 1915 seventeen local businessmen had been trained as volunteer motormen, even though not paid they were required to take over for a recognised duty roster. In May 1918, it was agreed to employ women as drivers. Six conductresses were immediately trained to drive.

Travelling Billboards

Advertising on tramcars could form an important part of their income, although there were many differences of opinion as to the desired style. In general 'company' cars made every possible space available, to the point where the advert could obscure even the route information, whereas Corporations and Councils often kept such adverts (where carried) to the between decks panelling. Initially many refused to consider any advertising but in the end even Sheffield despoiled their pristine paintwork. Income obviously varied, a small town might only earn enough cash from all its cars to pay at best only one driver's weekly wage, whereas a big city could find its weekly wage bill almost balanced. Broadside advertisements on London County Council trams (20 ft × 20 in/6.1 × 0.5 m) cost 25p each per week, this together with smaller panels elsewhere was expected to generate enough cash to pay for the cars' annual painting.

Generally, but not always, advertising was handed over to a contractor for a fixed fee per car for a number of years, transferring the problems to him for a lower profit. Before the days of television the value of advertisements which by sheer repetition must have sold the products well, must not be underestimated. Although bearing in mind the illiteracy of much of the population it is a little surprising more use was not made of ideograms. Anomalies could also occur and add to the charm of tram photographs. For example car 145 of South Metropolitan Tramways for years had an advertisement for Nugget Shoe Polish on one side and, as funds were not forthcoming, the other remained blank. On occasion some devil's imp led to bold lettering advising one to buy Nestles chocolate at one end and Van Houtens at the other. Weston-super-Mare, logically, advertised Fortes Ice Cream Parlour; Walthamstow, rather upmarket, favoured 'Dogs Love Vims', while London United Tramways regularly warned the onlooker to 'Take Bovril or take the consequences'.

Post-War Problems

After the war road-vehicle licences increased to a vast flood and one traffic problem for which trams were, totally unfairly, held to blame was that of traffic jams. As city after city abandoned electric transport so this fallacy became more and more apparent, for traffic jams seemed inescapable then and still are today. Indeed to some extent modern traffic problems can be laid at the door of tram abolitionists as the very presence of solid tramcars ensured some discipline among other traffic users, and their high capacity enabled passenger queues to be cleared very rapidly. It is true that when a tramjam occurred there were difficulties but these were normally handled by Inspectors or Regulators who had the power to turn cars back on a short working, effectively introducing a shuttle. It was almost an invariable practice for these men to be ex-drivers or conductors (many drivers, it must be remembered, were ex-conductors anyway) and vastly experienced. Their responsibility was onerous enough for there never to be many applications for the posts. Short working had one disadvantage and that was the necessity for the conductor to go forth and explain to the passengers that they would shortly be required to vacate their relatively warm and comfortable vehicle and to catch another. No matter where this befell, in vain did the conductor explain there was 'another one behind', for disbelief was often vehemently expressed. With, probably, a two or three minute headway between services there often really was another one behind . . . well, quite often anyway!

Other occasions when short working could be called for were road works when a shuttle might be run, terminating each side of the hole with passenger walking the gap or more probably a 'bumpover' (a temporary bridge of rails) would be constructed which being crossed at less than walking speed delayed services. A Regulator was responsible for the crews' well-being in so far as, certainly in later days, if no relief crew appeared at the appointed time and place they were likely to walk off and leave the car. If no crew was immediately available the car might turn short and work back to the shed or crews and cars be shuffled about like dominoes.

The era of the traditional tramcar was also the era of smogs, a coal smoke enhanced fog which was so bad that even in the 1950s a car often had to be guided by the conductor walking in front with a flare not because the tram could get lost but simply because the air was so thick and yellow that at night the driver could not see more than a few inches in front of him and abandoned cars (and, dare I add, abandoned buses) were dotted about. Delays were unbelievable and short working using lay-bys, crossovers or any other way round the problem was commonplace. Then again, in extreme conditions of snow or ice it might be possible to run a service over part of the line but not the whole. In early days when the snow was impassable for more than a day or so the Manager might authorise taking as many unemployed men (i.e. those in receipt of Parish Relief) as necessary, issuing them with shovels and putting them to work, a

converted car following up for use as a restroom and hot-soup dispensary. Anti-freeze was another possibility, even though being alcohol-based not all went on the rails, and right at the end continental-style electric point-heaters are believed to have been experimented with. One alternative was to use a combination of snow ploughs on a few cars and the normal track cleaning rotary broom; the sight of this thrashing along encrusted with snow and ice really was quite daunting!

Even the local populations could be confused by short working as stand-in route numbers often bore no resemblance to their full-length parents. Thus in Birmingham a 36 terminating at Stirchley (British Oak) was a 46! The 59, on the other hand was a short working of routes 2, 63, 78 and 79. Very many town transport managers assumed that the passengers knew where they were to begin with and ignored tourists requirements. Two examples from one city – Birmingham. Initially cars had only a route number fore and aft, with no destinations. Later they were fitted with boards on the side which gave the grandiose information 'To [or from] City', or at best the route title. Thus route 36 carried a board marked 'Pershore Road', utterly useless for a stranger! Virtually every town or city that had tramcars put what little information they gave in a different position, all too often relying on the indicator being clean and unfaded and the would-be passenger having spectacular eyesight.

Progress?

Why, then, did tramways fail? In cities like Birmingham and Glasgow the insidious propaganda put out by oil interests and the construction industry brainwashed very many councillors into believing that tramways, and tramways alone, caused all the traffic problems of the cities, and that tramways stood in the way of the great god Progress. In fairness to the councillors of that age, progress seemed to beckon with the chance to rebuild both bomb-damaged and outdated streets; but like opening a Pandora's box they let all the evils of greed and wanton destruction ruin these cities by continuing (in the case of Birmingham, even today) to destroy hundreds of years of building evolution.

In the case of Leeds and Sheffield a lack of vehicle builders prepared to undertake the provision of a new fleet undermined their City Fathers' morale, but in Sheffield at least the trams remained immaculate to the last for even the lowly tram crews never really believed 'our' cars were doomed – it seemed all wrong, like an appalling nightmare, to put them away for the last time.

To what extent tramways sowed the seeds of their own destruction will always be debatable; in some ways it was right for Birmingham to boast cars of the 301 class (built 1911) that had individually covered over a million miles, but by the end of their life (1950) those with open balconies were the very antithesis of progress. Belfast 'Standard' red cars of 1905 still appeared on the streets (albeit for football specials) in 1950, most not having been externally painted since the mid-1920s. Some Glasgow 'Standards' were in appalling condition towards the end with the metal repair plates (ostensi-

bly holding rotted wooden joints together), themselves separated from the rotten wood. Some panels would gape open as the car crossed Sauchiehall Street and then the flexing of the bodywork would snap them to, catching many a bairn's fingers.

Salford was famous for its weary machines which not only sparked from the overhead, but from underneath as the motor casings thumped the cobbles. A few also suffered from dropsy inasmuch as one platform was distinctly lower than the other, giving rise to the nickname of 'Humpty Dumpty cars'. In Rotherham they had most ingenious single-ended trolleybus-like cars which, built in 1934–5, were in the post-war period notorious for both their unreliability and appalling condition. It is said that one was found stranded with both its motors having dropped off and the unconcerned crew smoking and apparently waiting for some Fairy Godmother to carry them away.

By then though, despite Leeds' brave, if half-hearted, attempt to build continental pattern single-deckers, the die was cast and in the United Kingdom only by visiting Blackpool with its piquant mixture of modern-styled and historic vehicles can we still enjoy the full flavour of revenue-earning traditional British electric tramcars. The coming of ultra-modern Continental-style 'Light Rail' services is to be welcomed; the contrast of old and new will then be complete.

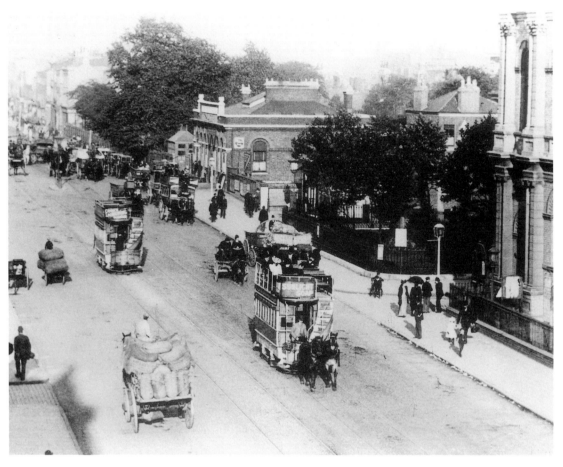

1. An animated scene showing North Metropolitan Tramways Company cars on the East India Dock Road, Poplar, 1904. This line opened in 1887 and was an immediate success. Unusually the North Met shared one characteristic with Glasgow Tramways insofar as although their cars were basically white, individual route colours were used; they were also the largest private company in London with, at their peak, 675 cars operating over 51 miles (82 km).

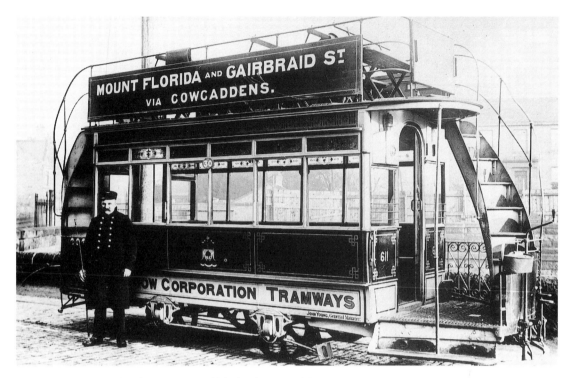

2. Horse tramcar No. 611 was one of 364 built to a Falcon (Brush) pattern by several builders between 1894 and 1898. It is not possible to say whether this was a new vehicle just out of Coplawhill Works (behind the photographer) or one already in service and simply wheeled out of the depot. The small oval plate bearing the number '30' on the centre window pillar prob- ably points toward the latter, because this is a removable service number to indicate the timetabling of that particular car on its route. The location is an interesting one from several points of view, and remains recognisable today – at least from the same angle as the photograph, which was taken prior to 1901.

3. Great Northern Railway (Ireland). Fintona horse-tram seen leaving Fintona terminus *en route* for the Junction railway station – it seems the chickens in the foreground are quite unperturbed by the advancing horse-tram! A great tourist attraction, the line did not close until 30 September 1959.

4. The Woolwich & South East London Tramways Company's lines were not quite as spectacular as their title, running only from Greenwich to Plumstead via Woolwich. Unusually for London, though, they were of 3′ 6″ (1.1 m) gauge. Opened 1881–2 car No. 4 is seen here approaching the Holy Trinity Church, Beresford Square, Woolwich, c. 1904, just before closure and electrification. The livery was pale primrose over blue.

5. The Cambridge Street Tramways Company started running services in 1880 and closed in 1914 without electrification. In this picture, car No. 8 waits near the railway station. Perhaps the company's only claim to fame lies in the use of one grossly overworked horse rather than the pair used elsewhere.

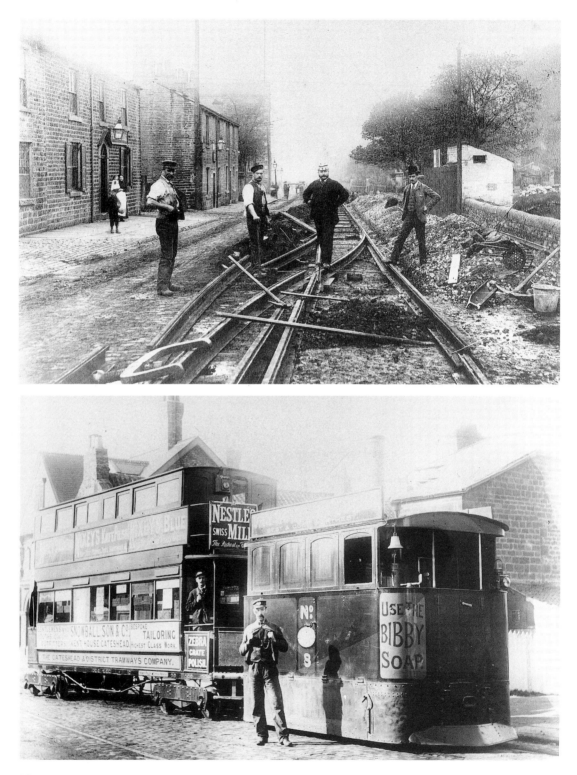

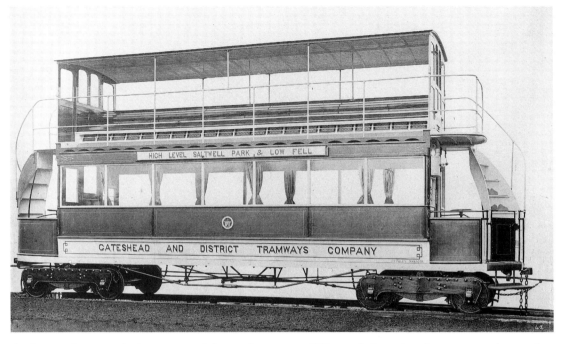

6. A rare photograph showing track laying for a steam tramway. Of 4′ 0″ (1.2 m) gauge, this length was laid near Rawtenstall, Lancashire, in June 1888. Apart from the onlookers and the workmen, in the left foreground is a 'Jim Crow' clamp used for bending rails, and on the right the profile of a short length of rail shows just how light this was in comparison with later equipment.

8. What is believed to be an original manufacturers photograph. The trailer is one of the same batch as that shown in fig. 7 prior to enclosure of the upper deck, showing the longitudinal bench seat and the lack of decency boards which made it impossible for any lady to ride upstairs. Photograph dated 1883.

7. The apothesis of the steam tramcar. Gateshead & District locomotive built by Black Hawthorn to Wilkinson Patents in 1884, and trailer built by Falcon in 1883, after enclosure in 1894. Interestingly on the back of this photograph is a note: 'This is a true photograph as my brother-in-law was the driver. M.J. Tweedy'. One suspects he was a man proud of his job.

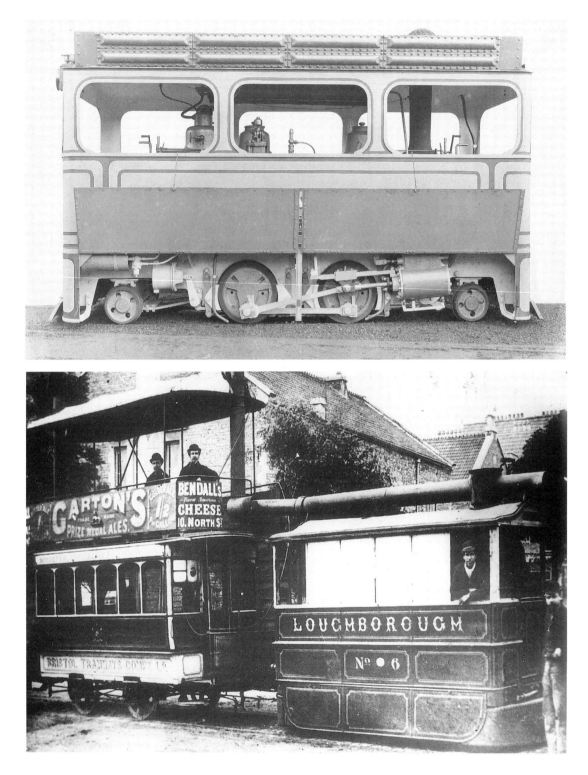

9. The ultimate evolution of the steam tram. Although export models were slightly heavier and stronger than those used in the UK, this Kerr Stuart manufacturers photograph of 1909 clearly shows the modified Stephenson gear, dual controls, condenser and skirts of a typical steam-tram power unit.

11. Falcon (Brush) Engine and trailer of Burnley tramways 1888. Most unusually, and with a singular disregard for the realities of the English climate, no top-deck covers were fitted, although passengers travelling upstairs paid a lower fare to allow for the dirt and cold. The engines used on the Burnley services were really scaled down locomotives with noisy, jangling but all enveloping iron plates added.

10. A most improbable arrangement of steam tram and trailer was tried by the Bristol Tramways Corporation for one year 1880–81 under contract with the manufacturer, Henry Hughes of the Falcon Works, Loughborough – hence the name on the locomotive. There was no provision for a condenser, the flexible coupling between chimney and trailer sooted up and caught fire, while the ride of the four-wheel converted horse-tram trailers was apparently liable to bring on sea-sickness. Hughes' works went into liquidation in 1881, being purchased by the company which eventually became Brush Electrical.

12. Photographed around the turn of the century this little tramway, of 8¾ miles (14 km), had the big title of the Giant's Causeway, Portrush & Bush Valley Railway & Tram Company. 1883-Wilkinson-built engine with a mixed passenger and goods train outside the tramway depot at Portrush. Photographs showing freight vehicles on this tramway are extremely rare although the Directors had hoped for considerable tonnage. Livery was cream with red lining and in the case of the covered car, extensive 'ornamental encrustations'. Opened 1883, steam-hauled services ceased 1914.

13. A primitive South Staffordshire Company's electric tramcar outside Pleck generating station just prior to the opening day, 21 November 1892. One of the earliest photographs of an electric car.

14. Dumbarton Tramways, Dumbuck terminus, 1907. This, believe it or not, was the main road to Glasgow. Seen when almost new, the late delivery of car No. 4 and her sisters forced a delay in the opening of the Burgh's tramways.

15. The primary excuse for the withdrawal of Glasgow tramcars was that they caused intolerable congestion of the roads. But in 1961–2, just one year from closure, they carried nearly 10 million passengers! The replacement buses did not and could not cope, but fortunately for the pundits the shipbuilding and allied trades died away and unemployed people do not require much transport. Prior to the First World War Jamaica Bridge was reputed to have 145 trams per hour passing over. At least a dozen are visible here in 1904 including one ex-horse conversion.

16. Colchester is a pleasant English market town situated in the pastoral lands of Essex. There were three railway stations, a town population of 12,000, a castle and Colchester was the headquarters of the Eastern military district, having cavalry and artillery barracks. The town also has

17. Merton terminus of London United Tramways (L.U.T.) and Nos. 168 and 296 show the original and enclosed top versions of L.U.T. type 'W' cars which were built in 1902 on Brill 22E bogies. Most later passed to London Transport and were finally scrapped in 1936. The vehicles in the background are L.C.C. owned, and the lack of through-running between Company (L.U.T.) and Council (L.C.C.), which bedevilled services for so long, meant passengers had to walk between the cars.

a Corporation run 3′ 6″ (1.1 m) gauge tramway network totalling $5\frac{3}{4}$ miles (9.3 km). The first service car ran 28 July 1904, the last 8 December 1929. There were 18 cars, all hard worked ascending the 1-in-12 gradient of North Hill: 9.20 a.m. on a glorious summer's morning.

18. North Bridge, Doncaster, 2 May 1910. This photograph probably depicts an official party about to board the first tram to cross the rebuilt bridge, the planned jamboree to celebrate this having been cancelled following the death of Edward VII. Centre-groove rails and roughened road surface for horses (to the right of the tram tracks) are noticeable as is the fact that one pole is ornamented, the other, presumably unfinished, still plain.

19. The maintenance of a tramway network was always conspicuous and placed a heavy debt burden on the operator, whereas omnibuses could be worked on in the peace and tranquility of a garage, safe in the knowledge that road upkeep was none of their worry. At various times the method of wire attaching to the overhead carriers has varied between soldering, clipping and a mechanical grip. Reaching the overhead seems not to have been a problem in Doncaster where this tower wagon was seen in the first decade of the century. The use of a horse as motive power was quite advanced, for many concerns relied on a hand-hauled tower plus ladders.

20. It is a legal requirement that trackwork must be insulated against current losses and that any tramway must be divided up into sections not exceeding half-mile. Electrical resistance is such that the ideal feeder wire to maintain the required 500 amperes at 2,000 yards (1,830 m) from the power station would have a cross section of 1.9 square inches (12.3 sq cm) of copper! Obviously this is impossible and by use of a negative booster a cable with a copper core of 0.4 inches (1 cm) across is acceptable. We do not know what wire is in use here for the cable cross section used in Bradford varied from 1.5 square inches (9.7 sq cm) – main feeders to the City Centre – to 0.3 square inches (1.9 sq cm) for normal 'satellite' feeders. As there are also fire alarm and pilot

21. The power for tramcars was normally to the order of 550 volts d.c. In early years the generators were coal-fired and in some towns the availability of a canal or railhead decided where the generating station went. In October 1897, Bradford's Valley Road works opened with six Siemens generators of 250 kw capacity each and six of 375 kw. No. 1 engine was photographed immediately after the opening.

cables present in the photograph one suspects the former. The workmen received between $2\frac{1}{2}d$ and $3d$ (2.5p) per hour (but were laid off in winter), foremen $4d$ (3.3p) and the Gaffer £300 per annum. Steam car and trailer on the right.

22. *En route* to the Aquarium and the narrow-gauge tracks of the Scarborough system await final adjustment and concrete infill during the winter of 1903–4. The 'Jim Crow' clamps in the right foreground were used to induce a curve in the rails while the tie-bars used to maintain gauge are visible. In the immediate foreground can be seen a fishplate joining two lengths together; as the holes wore oval under the pounding of the cars so the road would have to be dug up to repair the resultant dropped joint.

23. Salford and the mesh of overhead shows one reason why current collection by surface contact and conduit was assayed. Crossings of this type were overhead maintenance men's private nightmare, one de-wired trolley could bring the whole system to a halt. Photographed 10 August 1939.

24. Electric tramway operators being of a frugal nature tended to find uses for any odd bits of machinery that were lying around. City of Birmingham Tramways Corporation steam tram locomotive No. 10, built in 1884, was reasonably successful in passenger work and served excellently afterwards to tow a rail grinder. It cost £800 new, had a book value 20 years later of £1 and the running cost of 5*d* (4.2p) a mile track grinding (to reduce corrugations and flats at rail joints) was a very economical exercise. Two types of rail grinders using carborundum discs or plates were used, equating to the handy-person's rotary and reciprocating sanders of today, the former is shown here.

25. London County Council Tramways wheel-car No. 012, shunted out of the Charlton repair works by steam locomotive No. 1. Although the usual vans could cope with light materials, heavier trucks were required to move wheels and axles. Two of these (011 and 012) were built in 1909–10. As, for safety, it was many years before the tracks inside Charlton Works were electrified, an 0–4–0 saddle tank locomotive built by Andrew Barclay of Kilmarnock (No. 991) in 1904, was bought from Beckton Gas Works in 1908. It was replaced by petrol tractors in 1932 and scrapped in 1933. The electric car (right) is No. 158, class B, for staff transport; built in 1903, these cars were loathed by drivers and passengers. No. 158, a late survivor, was scrapped 1929.

26. Car 51 of the Gateshead & District Tramways Company was built in 1903 as a combined track cleaner (using chisel-like tools to clear the grooves) and water car. The water tank being rotten in 1925 she was renumbered 51A and converted to a track grinder and snowplough. Seen above the inspection pit at Gateshead's Sunderland Road depot.

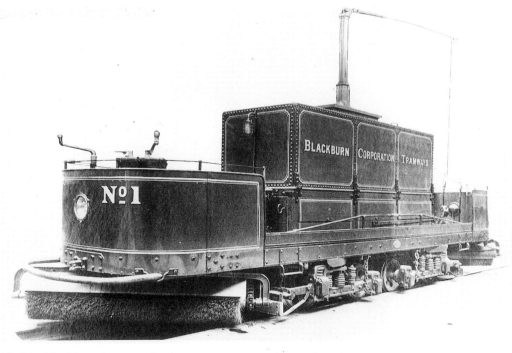

27 & 28. Blackburn's one and only maintenance car underwent many vicissitudes from its building by Hurst Nelson in 1900. It started life as shown here [27] as a combined water car (to lay the dust) and sweeper (to reduce horse-muck and other rubbish in and around the tram rails). As roads became tarmacadamed, requirements changed, and it was dismantled in 1908, parts – particularly the bogies and mainframe – being used to build the passenger-carrying, cross-bench single-deck car No. 88. Later, in 1914, a four-wheeled and very versatile permanent-way towing car was made from other parts. Photographed just after repainting in 1921 [28].

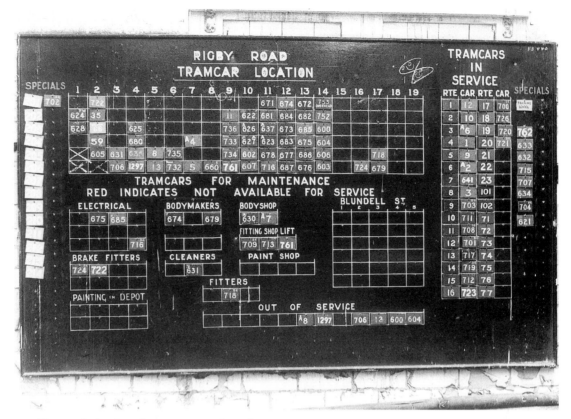

29. Kyotts Lake Road Repair Works of Birmingham Corporation Tramways showing the traverser at work. Traversers were excellent machines in workshops as they allowed a car to be moved to or from any road broadside on, thus eliminating the necessity for space-wasting pointwork. Photographed shortly after the closure of the system, No. 8 had the gloomy distinction of being the last operative tramcar in Birmingham. Built for the City of Birmingham Tramways in 1901, this car was numbered 505 in the B.C.T. fleet and converted to a rail scrubber or grinder in 1920 and ended its days as a tractor shunting cars around for breaking up, before succumbing itself in August 1953.

30. No electronic fleet controls were visible at Rigby Road depot of Blackpool Corporation Tramways, 1984, but similar boards were once found at every depot of virtually every tramway; apart from the 'Gaffer' knowing where the cars were, the crew could also be sure of their running road. At 4.30 a.m. on a winter's morning trams tend to look alike!

31a. In many ways it is a pity that today we are so blasé. This was not the case on 9 June 1898 when the line of the Halifax Corporation Tramways was opened between Old Station and Highroad Well. An estimated 4,000 people crowded Commercial Street to see the marvel of the electric tramcar. Somewhere in the boskage are the Lord Mayor, Lord Lieutenant and other invited gentry.

31b. A rather unusual decorated car inasmuch as it celebrates the opening not of a system or even one line, but of a joint service between two towns, Bolton and Bury. This is in fact Bolton car No. 40 standing outside the depot but the rocker panel has had the name covered up (20 May

32. The first electric tram arrives in Old Market Street, Bristol, 15 October 1895. On the left an almost redundant horse-drawn tram comes from Lower Castle Street; centre, the new posts carry the overhead wires; the eight new trams are lettered 'A', 'B', etc. to 'H'; Alderman Swaish stands on the top deck of the nearest tram, pointing; immediately behind him sits Alderman Dowling, both wear top hats and both became Lord Mayors. A count of heads shows about 750 visible, plus others out of sight, totalling 2,000 or more to view the great send-off.

1907). The almost fanatical local pride involved can be gathered from the appearance of the tramcar.

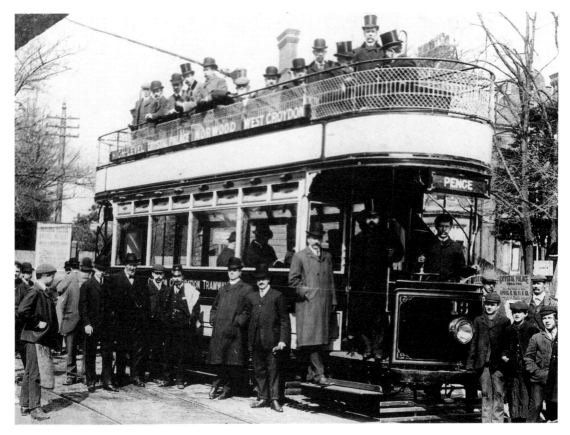

33. Before any tramway could be opened it was a requirement that a Board of Trade Inspector travel over the system, noting any defects. As examples, he might find insufficient clearance given against a pavement, stipulate speed limits and require that a type of lifeguard be changed. South Metropolitan car No. 13 in Thicket Road, Penge, with the Inspecting Officer, Colonel von Donop on the platform, 10 April 1906. Body built by the United Electric Car Company, on a Brush truck.

34.

GIANT'S CAUSEWAY
ELECTRIC TRAMWAY

THE WORLD'S FIRST HYDRO ELECTRIC TRAMWAY—OPENED 1883

TIME TABLE from 1st MAY, 1949

UNTIL FURTHER NOTICE

Tramcars between Portrush, Bushmills and Giant's Causeway will run as follows:—

WEEK DAYS			SUNDAYS		
Portrush to Bushmills and Giant's Causeway	Giant's Causeway to Bushmills and Portrush	Bushmills to Portrush	Portrush to Bushmills and Giant's Causeway	Giant's Causeway to Bushmills and Portrush	Bushmills to Portrush
10.30 a.m.	—	8.15 a.m.	—	—	—
12.30 p.m.	—	9.30 ,,	—	—	—
2.25 ,,	11.20 a.m.	11.30 ,,	—	—	11.30 a.m.
A3.20 ,,	1.20 p.m.	1.30 p.m.	12.30 p.m.	1.20 p.m.	1.30 p.m.
4.10 ,,	3.15 ,,	3.25 ,,	2.25 ,,	5. 0 ,,	5.10 ,,
5.15 ,,	A4.10 ,,	A4.20 ,,	X6. 0 ,,	6.20 ,,	6.30 ,,
X6. 0 ,,	5. 0 ,,	5.10 ,,	X7.15 ,,	—	—
AX7.30 ,,	A6.20 ,,	A6.30 ,,	—	—	—
BX9. 0 ,,	—	B8.15 ,,	—	—	—

A—Sats. only   B—Thurs. and Sats. only   X—Bushmills only   X—Bushmills only

SPECIAL EXCURSION TICKETS

Will be issued from Bushmills to Portrush Daily by all Tramcars at Fare of 1/2 Return, available for day of issue only.

SUBSCRIPTION MONTHLY AND WEEKLY TICKETS

Are issued at Reduced Rates, also Special Rates for School Children and Special Parties, on application to Tramway Office, Portrush.

Special Tramcars can be engaged on application.

Travel by Electric Tramcars, the best means of viewing the beautiful coast and enjoying the magnificent scenery.

NOTE.—This Time Table is liable to alterations, if found necessary, without notice from the Company.

The Company will not hold themselves responsible for Tramcars not starting at the times appointed, nor for delays that may occur on the road.

The Cars have special stopping places, indicated by sign, " CARS STOP HERE." Passengers are requested to meet the Cars at those places and are cautioned not to get on or off the Cars while in motion.

FARES.

	Single Fare	*Return Fare		Single Fare	*Return Fare
Portrush and Giant's Causeway ...	1s 9d	3s 0d	Bushmills and Dunluce Castle ...	9d	1s 0d
Portrush and Bushmills ...	1s 0d	1s 6d	Bushmills and Giant's Causeway	6d	—
Portrush and Dunluce Castle ...	9d	1s 0d	Portrush and White Rocks		
Portrush and Portballintrae ...	10d	1s 3d	Portrush and Golf Club	3d	—

*Return Tickets are available for One Month from day of issue.

G. F. MEARA, Engineer/Manager.

Telephone: Portrush 2318.

Portrush, 1st May, 1949.

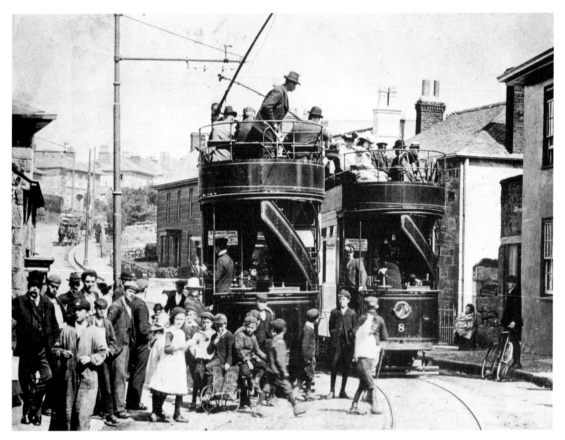

35. The Camborne & Redruth tramway was the only electric service operated in Cornwall and was opened for passengers in October 1902 with freight trams following in 1903. Closure for passengers came in 1927, mainly due to the depressed state of the mining industry in Cornwall, with men being laid off. 3′ 6″ (1.1 m) gauge, all the eight cars were built by Milnes with B.T.H. electrical equipment. Nominally seating 50, on football and gala days, 150 passengers were normal. Nos. 7 and 8 are seen at Pool Village crossroads in the summer of 1903 just after delivery. The fit of some components seems a little haphazard but no doubt trundling up and down the 3¾ mile tramway would bed them in well.

36. The back of this photograph carries the information that it was a 'treasured card of the electric tramcar which was the first to pass through Stourport on Tuesday, 3rd May 1898'. B.E.T. owned, the Kidderminster & Stourport Electric Tramway Company opened their line officially on 25 May with a 20-minute service. Basically the line was a country one with fallen leaves from trees more of a problem than other traffic. Parcels provided some part of their income including farm produce (eggs and vegetables) plus live fowl! The line closed 2 April 1929, the company then becoming solely an electricity supply concern.

37. Doncaster Corporation Tramways built their Oxford Street route rather unwillingly. Opened November 1903 with a 20-minute service, by May the following year trams ran only on Friday and Saturday evenings, the income being

£1 a month! The route closed on 18 May 1907 and we can, therefore, date this photograph of Camden Street between 1903 and 1907. The hats are magnificent and the cars, like the passengers, look beautifully clean, befitting their special working to the Co-op Gala.

38. The Light Railway Transport League (now Association) includes among its members most, if not all, of the famous tramway names, some of whom are seen here on their Annual Convention 15–18 April 1949. Photographed outside Blackpool's Rigby Road Depot before commencing their tour in cars 208 and 217, then still in more or less original condition with sunshine roofs, heaters and clocks.

39. By this date, 9 April 1938, an unrebuilt tramcar was a total anachronism, and yet Bristol, once Britain's premier seaport, kept these in service until 1941. The cause was the seven-year 'scrap-iron' clause in the Tramways Act; after the 1920s no shareholder would expend money to modernize equipment that might be compulsorily purchased for very little money. In the event the Great Western Railway purchased over 50 per cent of the shares in 1930, then transferred them to a bus company which, in 1937, sold the whole concern to Bristol Corporation. Bus-orientated, they promptly started to scrap the cars, the last running to this area, Hotwells, on 7 May 1939.

HENLYS PL IT

40. South Metropolitan Tramways suffered from difficulties with Croydon Corporation which effectively bifurcated their network. Four advertisements are visible here, all enamelled plates and all somewhat battered. Car 25, seen in Aurelia Road, of Type K was built in 1902 and like her sisters, disliked by drivers for the rough riding of their primitive Milnes girder bogies. Scrapped 1934.

41. Designated Type A, M.E.T. car No. 99 was built by Brush in 1905. Unusually the staircase consisted of two flights separated by a landing. Called the 'Exhibition' type they were designed with safety and convenience of passengers in mind, albeit at the cost of less seating in the tram. A really elegant tramcar, and the advertising is restrained; Black & White Whisky survives to this day, the Morning Post is now part of the Daily Telegraph. Car later renumbered by London Transport as 2457, scrapped by 1936.

42. Like most provincial company-owned tramways Camborne & Redruth relied on advertising for a good part of their income. No. 1 tram, groaning under its load of enamelled notices is standing at Camborne terminus in 1903. The driver is William Hampton and the conductor, holding an early Glasgow-pattern ticket punch, is A. Wallace. The curtains at the windows still remain. What a delightful time, when one could stand and wait for the photographer.

43. When this photograph of car 2 of the Weston-super-Mare & District Electric Supply Company was taken in 1935 the system had less than two years to run, closing 17 April 1937. By contrast with earlier years advertising revenue had almost gone, but the cars remained in generally good condition. The driver's blind spot caused by the staircase is very obvious and by 1937 it was no longer reasonable to expect any motorman to be exposed to all weathers through the winter. Locking Road Depot, Philip Maynard at the controls.

44. The 'best' tram (or 'best' anything) must be a personal choice, depending really on where you worked, how far it impinged on your personal life, whether you had good workmates and a dozen other factors. A Liverpool 'Green Goddess' perhaps (happy courting days), a London E1 (because you knew you could stop), Sunderland (such exhilarating rides) or shall it be the Glasgow Coronation? Not the (rightly) polished and cossetted museum pieces, but a workaday orthodox car here and there dented, perhaps a little rusty, could be a flat or two on the wheels, maybe even having seen her best days. But still a Coronation. Designed by a genius, profanely but skilfully built, worked hard in war and peace and still always a drivers' tram. The prototype 1141 was built (as they all were) at Coplawhill Works at a cost of £4,406 and entered service on 1 January 1937. She measured 34' 0" (10.4 m) long and 7' 3½" (2.2 m) wide, seated 65 passengers and weighed just 16 tons 12 cwt (16,870 kg). The designers gave drivers a seat, dipping headlights, a sunshade, stop and fog lights, trafficator arms, an electric windscreen wiper that worked and a good mirror. The passengers got modern lighting, an airy saloon, leather and moquette seats, and upstairs full-leather seats and curved roof lights; just like a seaside car! They rode on the sweetest of trucks, the E.M.B. lightweight. The production run was for 150 cars – it is said there might have been 500 – each costing £3,354 – a double-deck bus was then £1,895. No. 1285 was a wartime baby, completed in 1940, and is seen here at Dalmuir West on 12 June 1962.

45. Welsh townscape with trams in abundance. The use of a concrete trackbed ensures that the maintenance limit of the Corporation Tramways in Swansea are clearly defined *c.* 1900. Car No. 28 is bound for Morriston. On the left the horse-shoe sign bids you buy a 'Lucky Wedding Ring'. On the right the Cameron Arms Hotel has vacancies – for honeymooners perhaps!

46. Sheffield tramcars remained elegant and immaculate to their last day, 8 October 1960. One of the worst aspects of the closure of Britain's tramways in the 1950s and 1960s was not only the cessation of the most efficient, pollution-free form of bulk people-moving transport, but also the loss of all the accumulated knowledge of 100 years of tramway operation. Car 518 was one of the Jubilee class of cars built by Charles Roberts in 1950–1952 when, it seemed, traditional tramways in Sheffield had a future.

48. Southend-on-Sea tramways, Thorpe Bay. Pretty children, attractive fashions. Car 8 was shortlived being altogether too small (38 seats) but was just a year old in 1902.

47. Newcastle tramjam. Photograph taken in 1938 from the balcony of the Paramount (now Odeon) Cinema looking up Northumberland Street across the junction of Northumberland, Pilgrim, New Bridge and Blackett Streets. Car 195 was home-built in the Newcastle Corporation Tramways workshops in 1912. The system closed in 1950.

49. Rothesay is the principal town on the Isle of Bute. Were there any natural justice there would still be a tourist tramway operating on the island as there was between 1879 and 1949. Photographed well before the First World War, an electric car of the first series built at Preston in 1902 crosses over at Guildford Square. The object on the left-hand bottom corner was the famous and long-demolished Iron Fountain while the spire in the middle (St John's Church, Argyle St) was demolished in 1973. Transferring the tramcars from the mainland must have been interesting as necessarily they had to be ferried on barges from Greenock; an operation which must have given the contractor Rose & Marshall Ltd a few qualms way back in 1902!

50. The cable car was really quite elemental in principle and unbelievably complex in operation. The basic theme was of a moving cable travelling at 6–8 mph and working in a trough, to which a tramcar was attached or detached by means of a gripper, two jaws which grabbed hold of the cable. Obviously when a passenger wished to board the driver had to let go of the cable and apply his brakes. Corners were difficult and junctions diabolical. July 1894 and gripper car No. 8 waits at Telford Avenue, Streatham Hill, 24 years after the inception of the three-mile route and ten years before it was electrified. The cable was continuous, six miles long, powered by a steam engine. Licence discs very visible, uniforms lacking. The advantage of a separate 'dummy' gripper car was that the trailer could be horse drawn when required. This was both convenient for working through to Waterloo and necessary when cable repairs were required.

51a. By contrast Matlock Urban District Council saw the cable car as a means of ascending Matlock Bank with its maximum gradient of 1-in-5½. The ⅗ mile (1 km) long route was opened in 1893, and handed to the council as a gift five years later, being closed in 1927 in favour of buses. Photograph dated March 1893.

51b. The Great Orme Tramway runs from Victoria Station, Llandudno to Summit Station 679 feet (207 m) above sea level and is cable operated. Gradients are as steep as 1-in-4 and the lower section, which shares the road with rubber-tyred vehicles, winds and twists to the detriment of the cable. Here a maintenance man oils the cable rollers early one June day in 1985.

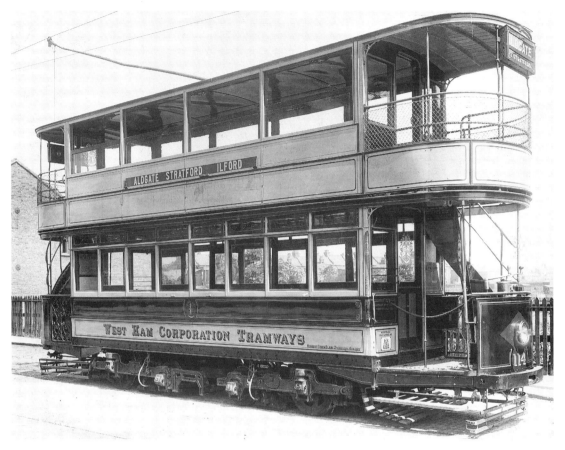

52. A Hurst Nelson 1911-built dual-fitted car, subsequently 320 in London Transport days and not dissimilar to the L.C.C. class E. Staircase layout is odd and the small lower-deck windows rather old-fashioned. The left-hand bogie is extended as a conduit plough carrier. The Corporation coat of arms is proudly etched in the glass of the saloon doorway.

53. Torquay was one of six British tramways to try surface-contact current collection and one of three to use the Dolter system. Mexborough (1907–8) and Hastings (1905–14) were the others, while Torquay lasted from 1907–11. Track laying during 1906 is seen here in the Strand with Victoria Parade to the right and Torwood Street to the left. The contact boxes are clearly visible, while the feeder cable is seen in the excavation in the foreground. The damage to, and area of, the road occupied are equally apparent.

54. Very many tramway concerns followed the chimera of battery electric traction as it promised the benefits of silent electrical transport without the necessity for expensive and complicated overhead wires. Seven of these five-ton (5085 kg) machines were built by The Brush Electric Engineering Company of Loughborough in 1889 to serve the four-mile (6.4 km) long Sandhurst (now Bendigo) and Eaglehawk line in Australia. They were 22 seaters, had 56 storage batteries and were a disastrous failure, surviving less than three months in service, a fate which generally matched that of their UK-based cousins.

55. Wolverhampton Car No. 65, seen when new outside Cleveland Road depot, was one of the last to be built for use with Lorain stud contact equipment. The Brill 21E truck necessarily has an extended frame to support the lifeguards clear of the contact skate. English Electric 'Preston' type of 1920, seating capacity 53.

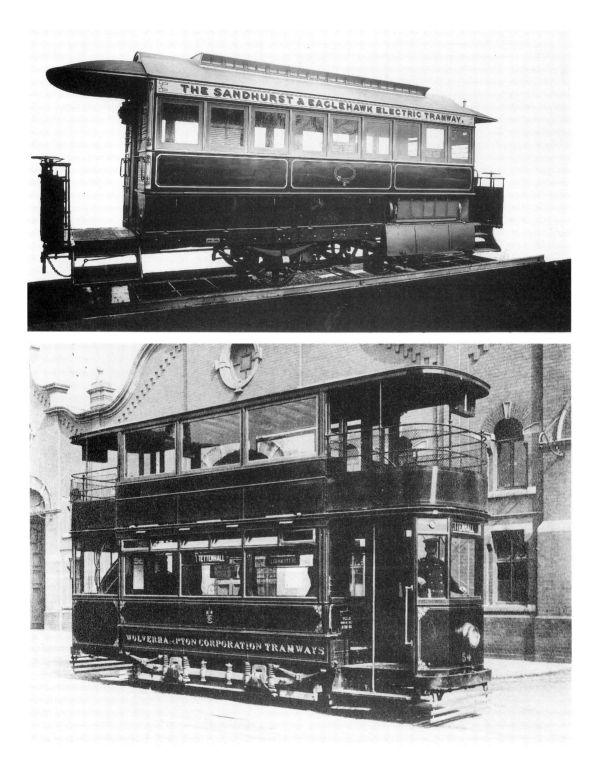

56. A dual-fitted (trolley pole and conduit) Class E1 car, running on conduit pick-up, stands alongside a usurping RT-type motor omnibus in 1949. Visible are the conduit inspection hatches and a power supply isolation box.

58. The Dublin & Blessington Steam Tramway purchased two enormous petrol-electric cars from Hurst Nelson & Company of Motherwell in 1915. Carrying 75 seated passengers they were powered by Aster petrol engines, with Westinghouse electrical equipment. The narrow centre entrance is clearly visible as is that twisting staircase which delayed boarding and alighting passengers. It seems the vibration was unbelievably bad, especially after a year-or-two's wear.

57. At first sight a very early and rather primitive London County Council Tramways' electric car, this is P1, one of a class of three petrol-electric cars converted in 1913 from horse cars. Equipment was by W.A. Stevens (of Tilling-Stevens fame) with the engine under one set of stairs and the radiator (visible here) under the other. Trials began in May 1913, they entered service on route 70 in July, but were withdrawn in December and the experiment abandoned.

59. The Morecambe area became famous for two tramway features, the last standard-gauge horse tramway in England and four petrol trams, of which this (seen *en fête*) was the first. Initially Company owned, the bulk of the network's $2\frac{3}{4}$ miles (4.4 km) were purchased by the Corporation and these 1911 U.E.C.-built Leyland-engined cars proved perfectly adequate for the remainder. They entered service 5 January 1912 and remained until the line closed 24 October 1924.

60. A study in tramcar architecture. Weston-super-Mare Tramway car No. 2, photographed in 1935. All the components of the classical Brush 1902-built car are visible. The paintwork was carried out by A.J. Deacon who mixed all his own paints from solid block. Basically crimson lake, lining out was gold, the bulkheads being a pale cream and the decency board grey. Brass handrails were kept polished despite the sea air and woodwork varnished annually.

61. The Belfast Street Tramway Company tracks eventually totalled $21\frac{3}{4}$ miles (35 km), with (in 1904) 171 double-deck cars and 34 ancillary vehicles, which included an ambulance; the ride on rails was no doubt smoother than over cobbles. Some of their cars are seen in High Street sometime in the early 1880s; the sun awning over the lower saloon windows on the nearest car provided an unusual touch.

62. The last of the standard 'red' type cars of the 1905 batch lasted until 1951 by which time they were used only on football specials as is No. 54 seen reversing at Windsor Grounds Crossover. Not having been re-painted since the 1920s she looks distinctly tatty. As long as Andrew Nance was General Manager (1904–16) he steadfastly refused to allow the driving platforms to be enclosed on health grounds, reasoning that open air and driving rain was good for the drivers.

63. The building of the McCreary cars (392–441) was authorized in 1934 and on arrival made the rest of the fleet look outdated. Seating 64

passengers the underframes were supplied by Hurst Nelson, the bodies built by the Service Motor Works, Belfast (392–442), and English Electric (392, 423–441). There were problems later with drooping platforms which twisted and caused leaks in the bodywork but they were a pointer to future designs. In the background, standing at Springfield Road terminus is a Chamberlain car No. 364 of 1930, Brush-built to traditional outline, but with leather seating, electric heaters and air brakes.

64 & 65. In 1921 Middlesbrough Corporation purchased nine new 64-seater double-deck cars from Hurst Nelson of Motherwell and numbered them 132 to 140. No. 132, austere and angular, is seen here prior to entering service while her sister 134 is seen later hard at work. The tramways ceased operation in June 1934 but only four of the cars saw further service, regauged from Middlesbrough's very odd 3′ 7″ (1.1 m) they went to Southend-on-Sea Corporation.

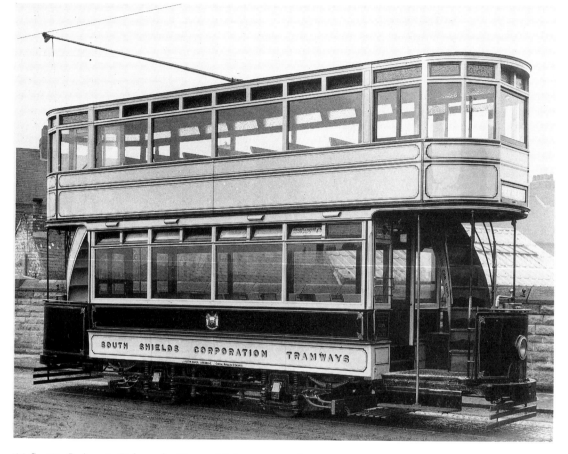

66 & 67. J. Austin Baker, the General Manager of South Shields Corporation Tramways, had the remit to carry quite extraordinary passenger loads at a reasonable fare and as these two cars show, he succeeded. The system opened in 1906 and closed 40 years later, when trams were superceded by trolley buses. No. 14 originated in 1906 as a standard U.E.C. car but was extensively rebuilt in 1928 with enclosed top decks, Smith Pendulum trucks, more powerful motors and new controllers. A seating capacity of 60 and a lively performance were attained. The ventilator advertisement encourages one to buy Brown & Polsons Cornflour, the blind reads 'Pier Head'. No. 49 (one of 18 to be named) was unique being almost wholly newly built in the Tramway Workshops in 1928–9. With a seating capacity of 61 she was neat and efficient. Unusually she carried an advertisement for the tramways services advising one to 'Ride the best way – SSCT' and the only decipherable ventilator appears to show passengers 'How to clean the teeth' together with diagrams.

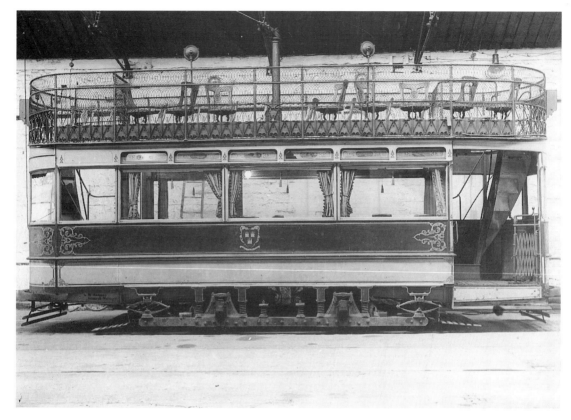

68a. Dublin United Tramways Company Directors' tram, built in 1901 by the company, was perhaps the most luxuriously fitted tram ever to run on any tramway system in the British Isles. The dashes had neither headlamps nor fleet numbers but carried a fixed destination display showing 'SPECIAL' at either end of the upper deck. It is seen here in Ballsbridge Depot (South Dublin) *c.* 1938.

68b. An interior view of this car showing the beautiful ornamental double bracket lamps, the exquisite wood carving of the vertical pillar and the horizontal moulding above the quarter-lights.

68c. One of the quarter-lights of which there were two above each of the three main windows on the sides. Different scenes of Dublin and district were painted on these lights, here artistic licence is obvious with no overhead visible and a six-wheeled horseless horse-car in the background. None the less with the sunlight behind them such ornamentation must have been magnificent.

69. Tramcar No. 21 of the Llandudno & Colwyn Bay tramroad was the last but one to be delivered, arriving from English Electric in 1920. Seating was available for 60 passengers and the closure of the system in 1956 was illogical indeed, for although in 1954 they operated at a loss of £3,000 no less than 2,697,994 passengers were carried. It is said closure was inevitable as a result of the machinations of the local Electricity Board, but one feels an actively tourist-orientated council might have done more to keep the service open.

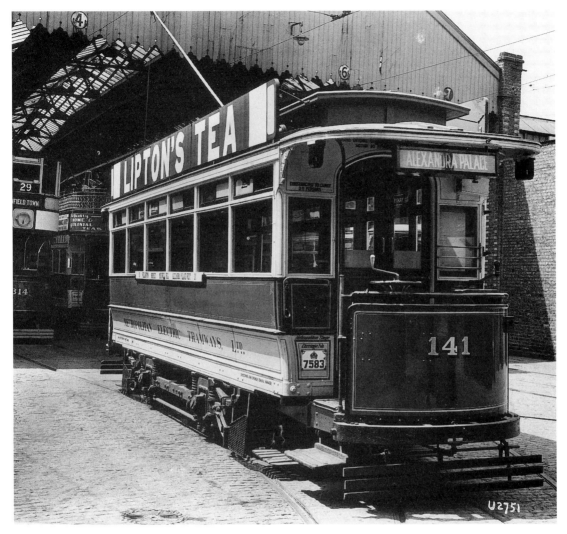

70. Metropolitan Electric Tramways car 141 was one of Type E, purchased in 1905 for use on the Alexandra Palace route. Interestingly, normal tramcars working to Alexandra Palace were not permitted to stop on the hill and four of this class were fitted with air-oil brakes to serve the patrons of the dance-hall situated half-way up. No. 141 became 2309 in the London Transport fleet and was out of use by 1938. In the background of this illustration are cars 314 (left) and 193 (right). No. 314 was of later build (1912) and became LTE 2246, while 193 of Type C/1 was built in 1908, became 2283, and like the others was out of service by 1938.

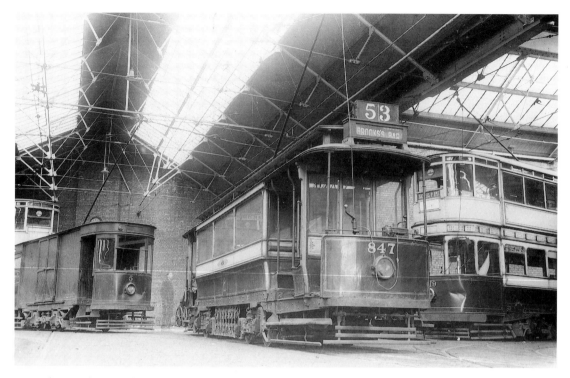

71. Three vehicles of the Manchester Corporation Tramways photographed in the late 1930s. No. 5 was home-built on a Peckham truck in 1905 as an express parcels car, although by the 1930s it had declined to use as a mundane, but vital, sand car. Normal practice with all large tramway concerns was to have one central sand drier in use, fresh supplies being sent out to sub depots once or twice a day as required. Thus the quality and free-running consistency of the sand used to give the wheels grip in poor weather conditions could be assured. Similarly 847 was used to carry sandbags from the early 1930s until 1948. Built by English Electric in 1921 she survived rather surprisingly after all the other single-deckers were disposed of in 1939. Locally nicknamed 'California' cars, the open ends were for smokers, only non-smokers used the saloon. A similar machine, 765, was rescued in the 1960s and is preserved. No. 579 was built in 1904 by Brush, seated 72, and was one of roughly 470 trams of generally similar outline.

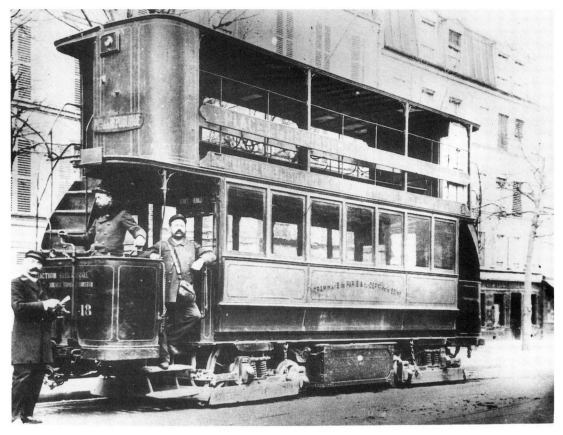

72. The basic details of virtually all European tramways were derived from American systems and American companies. This rather esoteric-looking machine was to be found in Paris in the 1890s and was powered by 'Traction Electrique, systéme Thomson-Houston', whose British cousins British Thomson Houston (B.T.H.) provided the tramcars in many a town. The curious blind front to these cars was commonplace on many French double-deckers.

73. If a tramcar can be ethereal this one built by Hurst Nelson for Durban Corporation Tramways must be it. The order totalled 16, the top covers were the first ever fitted by Hurst Nelson and the blinds furled under the roof were claimed to protect both decks from storms.

74 & 75. Car 35 [74] of the South Metropolitan Tramways was built at Preston in 1902 for the Gravesend & Northfleet Tramways Company and has the standard Dick Kerr interior of the period. The mirror adds a fancy touch to lighten the gloom of maple veneer ceilings and polished wood. Comfort was somewhat lacking although the pierced plywood backs of the seats have a pretty pattern! By contrast when car 342 [75] was rebuilt in 1924 from a L.U.T. type W Special Saloon of 1902 to type 52 as a one-man operated car it was wholly refurbished in the latest style complete with smooth easy-to-clean ceiling and updated lighting. The padded leather seating was a final touch.

76. Detail of a horse-tram axle box, bearing the once famous name of Starbuck who succumbed to competition before the electric age, not however before completing in excess of 800 tramcars during the horse tramway 'boom', indeed at one time four cars were being assembled every week. This casting dates back to 1871. Eventually the works were taken over by another famous tramcar concern, that of George F. Milnes & Co.

77. The basic use for a four-wheeled truck (or indeed a bogie) is to transmit the power of the motor or motors to the track, to provide adequate spinging for the car body above, and to give the driver good brakes to stop the tram. Logically the frame needs to be as long as possible to allow for a longer body above and hence increase the ability to carry passengers. The logical compromise is to make a semi-articulated truck which could 'bend' on tight track curves. The need to arrange simultaneously for constant power, braking and springing, as well as this 'bendability', led to many ingenious arrangements. By and large they did not work but this system, designed by James Lycett and George Conaty (Managing Director, Birmingham & Midland Tramways and Manager, City of Birmingham Tramways respectively), came nearest to success. Its complexity is self-evident.

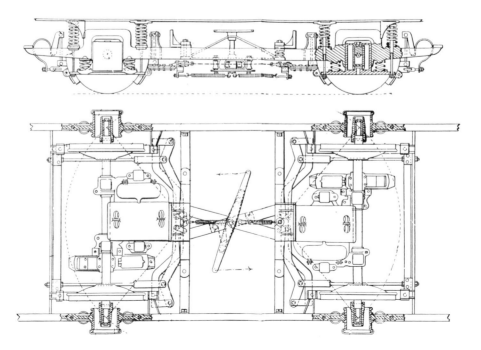

78. Leeds City Transport, photograph taken 12 April 1948. Car 240 of the Horsfield class, built by Brush for the City in 1931, seating 60. Car 272, later re-numbered 282 by Leeds, of the Manchester 'Pilcher' class, built by the Corporation also in 1931, seating 62, and sold to Leeds in 1947.

The next few illustrations have been brought together to show how gauge, livery and locale could decide the width of a tramcar and hence its capacity, comfort and ride. To give an example; Ipswich track gauge was 3' 6" (1.1 m) and because of narrow streets the Board of Trade stipulated a maximum car width of 5' 3" (1.6 m), with a result their Brush-built cars seated 50. Southend-on-Sea tracks were also of 3' 6" (1.1 m), cars were similar but by virtue of greater width seated 58. Incidentally most, but not all, of these photographs were taken on Light Rail Transit League (now Association) excursions when the cars were deliberately posed!

The notice between the cars was 'made available' for these enthusiasts' visits and reads 'Air Raid Shelter No. 2. Machine shop, stores, and sand drying depot.' In front of Car 240 is a dummy bogie used to bring back disabled cars.

79. Leeds City Transport, 2 April 1950, with two of the Middleton bogies of 1935, 258 being built by Brush and 267 by English Electric, old (left) and new liveries are apparent, 70-seaters. Still bearing its old London Transport number, 'Feltham' car 2099 was the first sent on trial prior to Leeds purchasing a number of them which were superfluous as 'Operation Tramaway' took hold in London. No. 2099 was eventually numbered 501 and like her sisters cost £500 with delivery at £235 for each car. Built 1931, seating 64.

80. A 'Feltham' car, built by the Union Construction & Finance Company Limited, was one of 100 built for use in London of which 54 went to Metropolitan Electric and 46 to London United Tramways. Deliveries of the class commenced in December 1930 and continued into 1931. Each cost £3,420. Three braking systems were provided, straight air, magnetic and hand. No. 2152 was 383 in the L.U.T. fleet and was allocated Leeds number 556. In this photograph she is still at home, the pole is down and the conduit slot in use.

81. Hockley Depot, Birmingham Corporation Tramways 1937. Visible are No. 183 of the 1906 'Radial' class, scrapped 1939; Nos. 632 and 602 of the 1920 '587' class, scrapped 1953 and 1950; and No. 533 of the 512 class, claimed by some drivers to be the sweetest running cars, which was not scrapped until 1952 after running over a million miles in service.

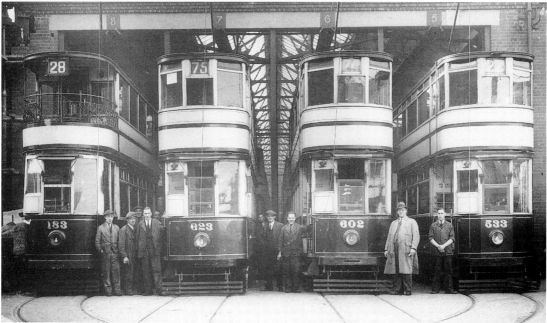

List of Streets and Places in Birmingham and District.	Which Car to take.	Central Depart and Arrive Termini.	Where to get off or on Car, and Right or Left turns to take for Street or Place required.	Ordin'y Fare.
				d.
FOR				
Homer st, Balsall Hth.	Moseley ..	High st or Hill st	Cars pass	1
§Homœopathic Hospital, 15, Easy row				
Hooper st, Dudley rd..	Dudley rd..	Edmund st ..	Cars pass	1
Hope st, Gooch st ..	Cannon Hill	Lr Temple st ..	Cars pass	1
Horse Fair	Selly Oak ..	Navigation st ..	Tram route	1
§Horse Mkt., Smithfield				
Hospital st, Summer ln	Handsw'rth	Colmore row ..	Summer lane, 2L ..	1
Howard rd,Coventry rd	Yardley ..	Station st ..	Cars pass	2
Howard rd, Hdswrth..	Perry Barr	Martineau st ..	Wellington rd, 3R..	1
Howard rd	Alcester lane	High st or Hill st	Cars pass	2
Howard st, Hampton st	Handsw'rth	Colmore row ..	Cars pass	1
Howard st, Smethwick	Soho ..	Edmund st ..	3R from terminus ..	1½
Howe st, Curzon st ..	Saltley ..	Martineau st ..	Cars pass	1
Hubert rd, Selly Oak..	Selly Oak..	Navigation st ..	Cars pass	1½
Hubert st, Aston rd ..	Aston Cross	Steelhouse lane	Cars pass	1
Hugh rd, Small Heath	Coventry rd	Sta. st or High st	Charles rd, 4L ..	1
Hume st, Smethwick..	Dudley rd..	Edmund st ..	Windmill lane ..	1½
Humpage rd, Bdsly Gn	Bordsl'y Gn	High st ..	Cars pass	1
Hunters rd, Hckly hill	Handsw'rth	Colmore row ..	Farm st, 1L..	1
Hunters vale, Hockley	Handsw'rth	Colmore row ..	Farm st, 2L..	1
Hunton hl, Gravelly h.	Erdington	Steelhouse lane	Cars pass	1½
Hunton rd, Gravelly hl	Erdington	Steelhouse lane	Hunton hill, 2 R ..	1½
Hunts rd, Stirchley ..	K's Norton	Navigation st ..	Cars pass	2
Hurst st, Smallbrook st	Balsall H'th	Lr Temple st ..	Tram route	1
Hutton rd, Handswrth	Perry Barr	Martineau st ..	Livingstone ro, 3L, 1L	1
Hutton st, Saltley ..	Washw'd H	Martineau st ..	Cars pass	1
Hyde rd, Ladywood ..	Ladyw'd rd	Lr Temple st ..	Cars pass	1
Hylton st, Vyse st ..	Handsw'rth	Colmore row ..	Vyse st, 1R ..	1
Icknield Port rd, Ldyw	Ladyw'd rd	Lr Temple st ..	Tram route	1
Icknield sq, Ladywood	Ladyw'd rd	Lr Temple st ..	Monument rd, 2L ..	1
Icknield st, Hockley {	Lodge rd ..	Edmund st ..	Cars pass	1
	Handsw'rth	Colmore row ..	Cars pass	1
Imperial rd, Bordesley	Bordsl'y Gn	High st ..	Cars pass	1
Inge st, Essex st ..	Balsall H'th	Lr Temple st ..	Cars pass	1
Ingleby st, Ladywood	Dudley rd..	Edmund st ..	Cars pass	1
Inglewood rd,Sparkhill	Stratford rd	Sta. st or High st	Cars pass	1
Inkerman st, Aston Newtown	Perry Barr	Martineau st ..	Cars pass	1
Inkerman st, Vauxhall	Washw'd H	Martineau st ..	Duddeston mill rd, 2R	1
§Inland Revenue Office, Paradise st				
Institute rd, Kings Hth	K's Heath..	High st or Hill st	Cars pass	2
*Iron lane, Stechford ..				
Irving rd	Erdington	Steelhouse lane	Wheelwright rd ..	1½
Irving rd, Horse Fair..	Selly Oak ..	Navigation st ..	Cars pass	1
Island rd, Handsworth	Handsw'rth	Colmore row ..	Cars pass	2
Islington row, Five W's	Ladyw'd rd	Lr Temple st ..	Tram route	1
Ivor rd, Sparkhill ..	Stoney lane	Station st ..	Cars pass	1
*Ivy House ln, Hall Grn				
Ivy lane, Lawley st ..	Bordsl'y Gn	High st ..	Cars pass	1
Ivy rd, Stirchley ..				
Ivy rd, Handsworth ..	Handsw'rth	Colmore row ..	Whitehall rd, 1R ..	1
Jackson rd	Alum Rock	Martineau st ..	3R from Terminus..	1
Jaffray Hospital ..	Erdington	Steelhouse lane	Jaffray rd cont'd ..	2
Jaffray rd, Erdington	Erdington	Steelhouse lane	Cars pass	2
Jakeman rd, Balsall Heath	Balsall H'th	Lr Temple st ..	Cars pass	1

H-I-J 40 Official Tramway and Street Guide to Birmingham.

* No Tram service near this Street or Place at present.
§ This Street or Place is situate in the immediate centre of Birmingham.

The information given on blinds and street furniture if it's going to work must be clear, comprehensive and kept clean.

82. Southport Standard of 1926, photographed 1965. Single line, some lettering squashed.

83. Birmingham was always at the forefront when it came to good passenger information (although their blinds were totally unhelpful) and the 'Official Guide' exemplifies this.

84. When originally opened the Balby line of the Doncaster Corporation Tramways terminated at this shelter at the junction of High Road and Oswin Avenue, the tracks ending in a 'Y' arrangement on either side of the building. Modern thought on British Rail is that shelters are not required for passengers as there are so many trains and yet here, on a service with an eight-minute headway, a shelter was provided as a social amenity. On 4 February 1915 the Balby route was extended to Warmsworth and the shelter, which had already needed to be locked at certain times due to vandalism, was removed elsewhere.

85. The original of this photograph, taken in the first decade of the century, carries a note on the reverse: 'This is the centre of town [Rochdale]. If you were here you would see it crowded with people, they all walk round that piece in the centre of the cars. It is commonly known about here as the 'monkey rack' or 'The Slab'. You can catch a car for all the routes there, and in the middle you will notice a building – that is where the tram conductors take their money.' It was, in fact, a combined office and toilet block known officially as Butts Island, opened 1907. It also served as that most vital aspect of tramways, the shelter: somewhere to rest a while, somewhere for a romantic tryst or merely somewhere to wait for a tram!

86. Newly outshopped from the Central Car Repair Works, Charlton, and still minus lifeguards, London Transport car No. 290 was saved from the wreckers torches. As West Ham No. 102 she was originally built in 1910 and had the unusual feature of six narrow opening windows per side in the lower saloon but then, as now, arguments arose over which should be open and when. In 1921 she was rebuilt as shown here, with the Peckham 'flexible' axles, which were suffering from wear, fixed as a normal four-wheel truck.

87. Bexley Urban District Council (U.D.C.) Tramways was a long title for a five-mile (8 km) long line. The story of the cars used by the Council is complex, and complicated by the fact that Bexley cars operated over London County Council rails to Woolwich while at the same time

Erith U.D.C. and Dartford U.D.C. cars operated into Bexley. In 1917 to make matters worse Dartford's cars were destroyed by a fire and Bexley provided replacements. In total 17 ex-L.C.C. class B trams were purchased by Bexley and six hired. Which were which is debatable, but this car was built in 1903 on a Brill 21E truck, and after passing to London Transport received the suffix 'C'. This photograph can therefore be dated between 1 July 1933 and mid-October that year when 20 was scrapped, having however, outlived her L.C.C. sisters.

88. Huddersfield Tramways. Route 7 at Ainley's Summit and car 103 nears the end of her climb from the valley, 1938. Magnificent scenery but a hard road for a tramcar.

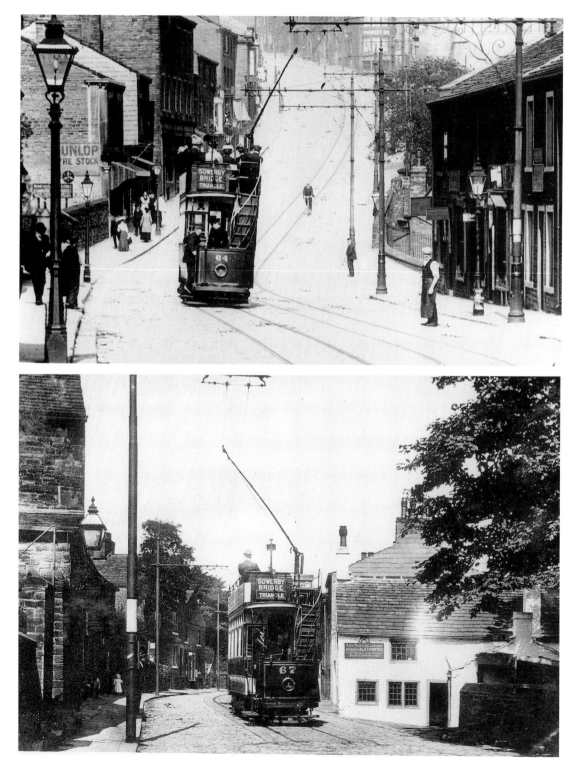

89. Halifax tram No. 64 on the Triangle route gets ready for the ascent from Wharf Street, Sowerby Bridge to Bottom Brow *c*. 1902. The Achilles Heel of a route like this were the long lengths of single track and often inconveniently located passing loops.

90. And at the Triangle terminus of the same route car No. 67 loads, *c*. 1903. A sylvan country scene, far removed from Wharf Street.

91. Cardiff tram No. 20 was already in rough condition when this photograph of St Mary's Street was taken, 22 August 1949. Taken over by the Corporation on 1 January 1902, the horse trams vanished after 26 July 1902 and although part of the electrified system was abandoned by 1939, nevertheless the last public service was not until 19 February 1950. Unusually, at the time of the photograph, a pay-as-you-board fare collection system was in force – a penny took you anywhere: simply and economically.

92. Described in 1831 as 'this magnificent canal' the 35-mile (56.3 km) long Forth & Clyde was opened on 28 July 1790. It was closed by Act of Parliament, 1 January 1963. Whether this act of official vandalism was greater than the destruction of Glasgow tramways is debatable but was it coincidence that the tramways died the previous September? At Dalmuir after much procrastination between the folk of Dumbarton and of Glasgow, a lifting bridge was built to carry the line of the tramway over the canal. It was formally opened on 10 February 1915 and from the following morning the terminus for Glasgow and Dumbarton cars became Dalmuir West at the old Burgh Boundary. Through running was not encouraged as apportionment of the fares was thought to be impossible. Both the passengers and the smartly uniformed motorman enjoy the twin pleasures of a tramway and a canal in Standard car 1124 on pleasant day in April 1954. All is now gone.

94. The traditional tramscape of the 1920s is exemplified by Forster Square, Bradford. All the elements of the period are visible, from fashion to the cars, and from the setts in the foreground to the double-decked tramcar grinding towards the photographer.

93. A most unusual scene in Doncaster as the conductors of two cars swing the booms round prior to their return journeys. Normally termini had automatic reversers but here at Station Road there was insufficient room, Car 28 is returning to Hexthorpe and the stationary car in the background is *en route* to Warmsworth. Photograph *c.* 1926. Car 28 was U.E.C.-built in 1913, seated 56 and was scrapped 1931 while the Warmsworth car of 38–47 series was built in 1920 by English Electric, seated 66, and lasted until 1935.

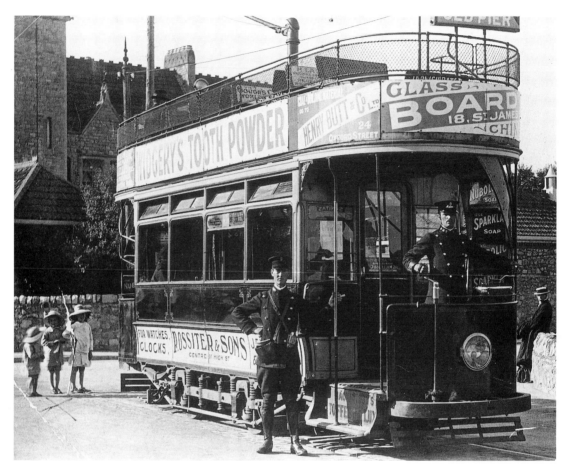

95. In 1920, the tramcar was still quite respectable and it was not difficult to let virtually every square inch of visible surface for advertisements. The entry step, reverse of the stair-risers, glass ventilators and even the backs of the swing-over seats upstairs recommend ways of lightening your pockets, albeit mainly local products. Photograph taken at the Sanatorium terminus, top of Quantock Road, Weston-super-Mare.

96. Camborne & Redruth Tramway staff at the depot in 1905. With the exception of two, the names of all the men are known. Obviously too many to list, but the rear row are conductors, the centre row basically motormen as are those in front. S. Ward, the Inspector, is standing on the extreme left.

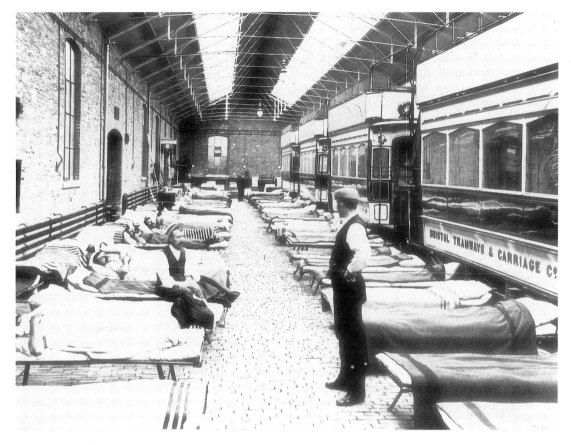

97. In 1901 the Bristol Tramways & Carriage Company suffered from a labour dispute and threats were made by strikers and anarchists that the trams would never run again. At Brislington Depot (and elsewhere) rather than have their loyal employees run the gauntlet of quite violent strikers and, one suspects, to protect the cars, the men were provided with beds beside the trams. When the troubles were over the 'loyal servants' received silver medals and varying bonuses according to their grade, two shillings (10p) a week for senior staff, one shilling (5p) for drivers and sixpence (2.5p) for conductors.

98. The number of volunteers to serve in the army so depleted Bristol's available manpower that services were drastically cut until 1 January 1917 when a 'mummeration of conductresses' was heard at Horfield Depot. Aged 18–25 the first 25 are seen here, receiving after training £1.3s.0d for a 54-hour week (6 days of 9 hours).

99. Parcels services were a source of consider-able income to many tramway concerns and sending it by rail ensured a prompt, efficient and, above all, secure service. Parcels car No. 1 of Manchester Corporation Tramways is seen 17 February 1905. One feels would-be muggers would hesitate to tackle the driver!

100. Very little is known about this photograph other than that it is of a Croydon Tramways car and is decorated in aid of the widows and dependants of men who fell in the Boer War. The passengers may be some of these women together with delegates of the organizing group.

101 & 102. When members of the Royal Family were known to be about to visit a town, staff members and management would get together to produce an illuminated car which would then tour the various lines of the network. [101] King George V & Queen Mary, Oldham, 12 July 1913. [102] King Edward & Queen Alexandra, Leeds, 7 July 1908: a tram which utilized '3,000 electric lights and 150 horse-power to run it'.

103. It is difficult for anyone much under fifty to appreciate the fervour with which British youth marched off in 1914 (and slightly less so in 1939) to do battle with the enemy 'over there', but after the first half-million or so were killed and those battered about began to appear (the worst being kept hidden in asylums) then recruitment tailed off. No Government wanted to introduce conscription so various other techniques to winkle out volunteers were tried including this tram which rumbled around Dumbarton in 1915 calling for men to join the 9th Argyll & Sutherland Highlanders. Whatever its direct success many tram crews joined up, and to such an extent that services, already overloaded, had to be cut, despite employing retired drivers and many ladies.

104. It was long a practice in Middlesborough to hold an annual Charity Carnival. When hospitals were dependent upon subscriptions from private individuals, companies and, possibly, a donation from the rates, the proceeds of such a carnival were greatly welcomed. The 'H' and 'T' letters are lost in this 1925 photograph as red was not accepted by the film. Car 50, built 1898 by Milnes and cut down to single deck 1911. The bogies are Peckham maximum traction cantilever of a pattern only used by Middlesborough.

105. 11 March 1948 and Leicester Corporation Car 60 stands in Groby Road. In those days, for safety, you put your money into Government schemes much as one does Building Societies today but apart from National Savings – 'make it a grand National Savings week and fight the crises with Savings' – there was to be a Schools Concert on Friday, 13 March, and you were exhorted to visit the Civic Exhibition at the Museum & Art Gallery.

106. An unusual excuse to ornament a tramcar came in the summer of 1908, when the South Parade Pier was re-opened by the Portsmouth Corporation, following a disastrous fire four years previously while in private hands. Numerous extra trams were run on these services which passed the Pier and No. 80 was used as a mobile and highly effective advertisement. The word in lights on the decency board is 'Success'.

107. Guernsey car No. 8 decorated for, and winning first prize in the 'Battle of the Flowers', probably in the late 1920s. Although carrying over a million passengers a year in 1931, in 1934 losses were escalating and the service finished 9 June that year. It was unfortunate for the Directors of the Guernsey concern that they were relatively isolated as No. 8, an 80-seater built by Milnes in 1896, had to be rebuilt almost as soon as she arrived, the 'Eight feet wheelbase truck now fitted to her is unserviceable' – just 6 weeks after delivery. The 'Battle of the Flowers' was probably her finest day.

109. Liverpool's No. 814 shows extensive damage as a result of enemy action during the night of 21–2 October 1940. She was repaired and returned to service.

108. Bradford and car No. 73 leaves Town Hall Square on Route 1 to Victoria Square one day in 1942. The Town Hall is the rather grand building in the background, while short 'utility' skirts, long queues, military uniforms, masked headlights, white bands on the wiring standard and the white painted bumper (for visibility) all show war's effect. During this period, too, photography was frowned on and illustrations are rather rare.

113

110. The Halifax combination of tall, narrow gauge tramcars, steep hills and very tight radius curves both inhibited technical advancement and was the cause of a number of accidents. No. 94 failed to complete her journey to Shelf on 1 July 1906.

111. Car No. 26 of the Huddersfield Corporation Tramways (left) was built by B.E.C. in 1902 and subsequently fitted with a Milnes Voss lightweight top cover. The driver, meanwhile, remained totally exposed to the weather. On 3 March 1906 following a brake failure she left the rails and ended up leaning on a house wall at the junction of Newsome Road and Colne Road, Huddersfield. No. 35 was delivered from the same maker in the same year and design differences abound, including the staircase and canopy above the driver. Oddly enough while 26 was later rebuilt with a modern roof and enclosed driver's cabin, 35 remained as shown throughout her life, being broken up in August 1933.

112. On 22 May 1915 car No. 89 of the Halifax Corporation Tramways ran out of control and overturned below Lee Mount. This view shows all too clearly the overhang at each end of the car and the narrowness of the truck on 3′ 6″ (1.1 m) gauge rails.

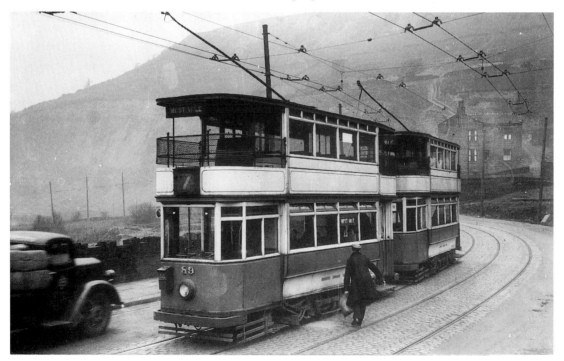

113. On 5 April 1939 car No. 96 of the Hudders-field Corporation Tramways became de-wired at Ainley's Bend. As it was impossible to free the boom with the bamboo re-wiring pole the follow-ing car, No. 89, is preparing to push 96 forward and the driver is sanding the track in readiness for this move. The letter-box on the rear of 89 was a common feature and provided a useful service. Trolleybus wires already *in situ* for the replace-ment service.

114. Please park prettily – not as car No. 2 of the Weston-super-Mare Corporation Tramways has done on the Locking Road. 22 June 1934.

117

115. Ramsgate, 3 August 1905, Isle of Thanet Tramways. Car No. 41 was damaged beyond repair in this accident when she came down Madeira Walk out of control in the rain and fell 32 feet (9.8 m) over the cliff. The driver, who was seriously injured, had only been a motorman for nine days. The design of the tram was such that the handbrake had locked the wheels and the slipper brake mechanism was so worn as to be totally ineffective. Although it was said 340,000 journeys had been made along Madeira Walk the Inspector, Colonel von Donop, expressed considerable surprise that the sanding gear designed to give more bite on the track was so aligned that the sand did not fall on the rails when the car was going round a curve.

116. On 1 June 1906 Swindon Tramways were to have one of the worst tram accidents on record when car No. 11 left Wood Street heavily laden with many standing passengers. On the 1-in-4 gradient down Victoria Road the car ran away, derailed near the Town Hall, fell over and slid along. Five passengers were killed, 30 injured, some seriously and, almost unbelievably, it was found that the Corporation was grossly under insured. Domestic rates were increased to pay the compensation. The cause was a disastrous braking system and poor maintenance. The Manager resigned, the motorman was downgraded and various other personnel were sacked.

117. Even at night advertising is valuable. It is also true that watching Blackpool's illuminations on an autumn evening can make 'Fisherman's Friend' (a type of throat lozenge) absolutely vital. The Western Train at dusk, 20 September 1984.

118. Pure nostalgia. No. 622 shows the glory of a London tramcar as she waits at Charing Cross *en route* to Wimbledon 1937. Built by Hurst Nelson in 1906, L.C.C. 'E' class. Scrapped 1938.

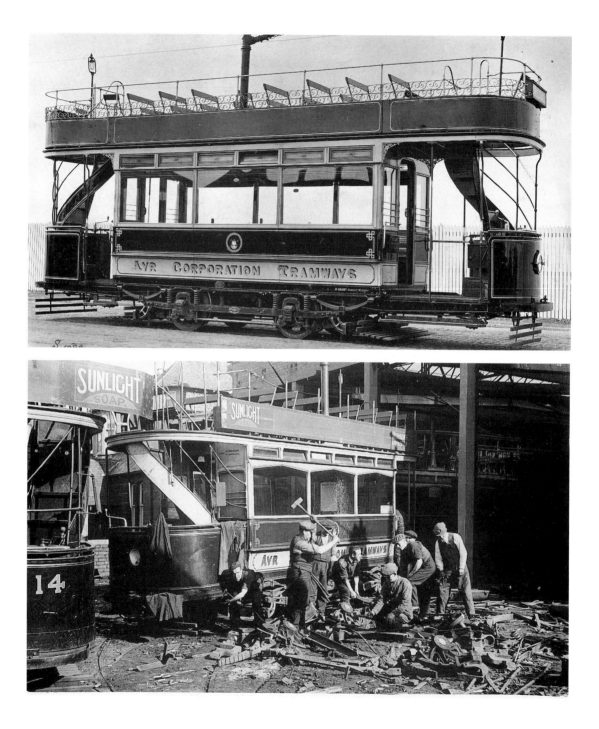

119 & 120. Nos. 211 and 212 of Ayr Corporation Tramways were built by Hurst Nelson in 1913 and designed to give a free unimpeded passenger flow via the additional exit under the stairs. Too narrow to be of much use the end result was a loss of seating capacity and an unbelievably draughty driving position. They were fitted with top covers in 1920 but short-lived through no fault of their makers, being scrapped in 1931 when the Ayr system closed.

121. When a tramcar reached the end of its life then it was right and fitting it should be burnt. But too often cars were broken up, not because they wore out, but because local or national politics decided they must go. It was said that the tram was outmoded and when it went with it would go traffic congestion and road accidents. Leeds Pivotal car 434 awaits burning at Torre Road depot, 1953.

122. When Birmingham got rid of its trams in 1952, they did not merely tar over the tracks and re-use the poles for lighting but with almost indecent haste eliminated almost all signs of their ever having been tramways. Whether the concrete, rat-infested subways are better than open streets is debatable, but there was no gainsaying progress in the 1950s!

123. To keep out the rain nearly all roadside tramway poles were finished with a neat finial. This is all that remains of the wiring along Pebble Mill Road, Birmingham.

124. Blackpool's cars still work up and down through the summer, albeit on a truncated system, but they are always under threat from the privatized bus companies with one at least having the avowed intention of running the trams off the road. The simple fact is that they do lose money and the same type of people who destroyed Sheffield's trams would dearly love to see Blackpool's go. But think how much poorer Blackpool and the country would be.

125. On the face of it a period piece but actually the Tramway Museum, Crich, in 1984.

Index to illustrations

Note: with the exception of London, illustrations are indexed under the name of the town or city; because of its growth the concerns operating in what is now 'London' are shown individually.

Ayr 119, 120

Belfast 61, 62, 63
Bexley 87
Birmingham 24, 29, 81, 83, 122, 123
Blackburn 27, 28
Blackpool 30, 38, 117, 124
Bolton 31b
Bradford 20, 21, 94, 108
Bristol 10, 32, 39, 97, 98
Burnley 11

Camborne & Redruth 35, 42, 96
Cambridge 5
Cardiff 91
Colchester 16
Crich, National Tramway Museum 125
Croydon 100

Dartford 87
Doncaster 18, 19, 37, 84, 93
Dublin & Blessington 58
Dublin 68a, b, c
Dumbarton Frontis 14, 103
Durban (S.A.) 73

Fintona 3

Gateshead 7, 8, 26
Giants Causeway 12, 34

Glasgow 2, 15, 44, 92
Gravesend & Northfleet 74
Great Northern Railway (Ireland) 3
Great Orme 51b
Guernsey 107

Halifax 31a, 89, 90, 110, 112
Huddersfield 88, 111, 113

Isle of Thanet 115

Kidderminster 36

Leeds 78, 79, 102, 121
Leicester 105
Liverpool 109
Llandudno & Colwyn Bay Cover 69
London County Council 17, 25, 50, 56, 57, 87, 118
London Tramways (Cable) 50
London Transport 79, 86, 87
London United 17, 75, 80

Manchester 71, 78, 99
Matlock 51a
Metropolitan Electric 41, 70, 80
Middleborough 64, 65, 104
Morecambe 59

Newcastle 47

North Metropolitan 1

Oldham 101

Paris 72
Portsmouth 106

Ramsgate 115
Rawtenstall 6
Rochdale 85
Rothesay 49

Salford 23
Sandhurst (Bendigo) & Eaglehawk 54
Scarborough 22
Sheffield 46
South Metropolitan 33, 40, 74
South Shields 66, 67
South Staffs 13
Southend-on-Sea 48
Southport 82
Swansea 45
Swindon 116

Torquay 53

West Ham 52, 86
Weston-super-Mare 43, 60, 95, 114
Wolverhampton 55
Woolwich & South East London 4